DRUMCLIFFE

The Church of Ireland Parish in its North Sligo Setting

by

Stella Durand

ISBN 1 873437 19 6

Published by **Drumlin Publications,**
Nure, Manorhamilton, Co.Leitrim, Ireland (072) 55237
Designed by Daragh Stewart
Printed by Colour Books

ACKNOWLEDGEMENTS

The author acknowledges with humility and warm gratitude that she could not have managed without the help of many people. She is particularly indebted to the Staffs of several libraries - Armagh Public Library, The Berkeley Library Trinity College Dublin, Boyle Library, The Digby Estate Office Sherborne, The Irish Architectural Archive, The Lecky Library Trinity College Dublin, The Governors and Guardians of Marsh's Library, The National Archive, The National Library, The Representative Church Body Library, Roscommon County Library, Sligo County Library, Trinity College Manuscript Room, Trinity College Map Library and The Yeats Society.

She is also exceptionally indebted to a few individuals who gave her unstinted time and attention: Frances-Jane French, Canon Ian Gallagher, Sir Josslyn Gore-Booth, Sylvia Lawson, Felicity McNab and Prionsios O'Duignean.

She is deeply grateful for the special help received from Sir Christopher Coote, Dr. Don Cotton, Patricia Cunningham, Brian Curran, Margaret Hedge, Rosaleen and Tom Holland, Bernard McDonagh, Joe McGowan, Aidan McKeown, John McTernan, Dr. Kenneth Milne, Bertie Monds, Dr.Raymond Refausse, and Mary and Martin Timoney.

She also acknowledges the invaluable help received from Dr. Alan Acheson, Cecil Barber, Jill Barber, Jim Barber, Dr. Daniel Beaumont, Roland Blennerhassett, Eileen Bligh, Basil Buchanan, Alfie Butler, Father John Carroll, John Corcoran, Jim Cunningham and family, Theresa Daly, Ernie Donaghey, Pamela Donaghey, Diana Duff, Joyce Enright, the late Ena Ewing, Erica Fairfax-Lucy(nee Loane), Aubrey Flegg, Canon W.E.C.Fleming, Gerry Foley, Hilary Gallagher, Annie and Dan Gilmartin, Eirenice Gore-Booth, Caroline Hamilton, Brian Haran, Canon Robert Hayman, Mary Heenan, Revd Ian Henderson, Tom Holland, Dermot James, David Johnston, Charles and Christa Jones-Henry, Helen Kerrin, Max Kilroy, Sheela Kitchin, Mary L'Estrange, Kitty McConkey, Tommy McGowan, Owen McIlroy, Sandra McIlroy, Stella Mew, Stella Mikhail, Revd Alan Mitchell, Dr. Desmond Moran, John Mugan, Drummond Nelson, Stephen Noone, Noni and Sara O'Beirne, Father Colman O'Clabaigh O.S.B., Frank O'Connor, Carolyn O'Laoire, the O'Rourke family, Norbert Platz, Nicholas Prins, Dr. Paddy Quin, Revd Noel Regan, Paddy Rolleston, Brendan Rooney, Grant Schofield, George Siggins, Dean Maurice Sirr, Martin Waters, Dr. Hugh Weir, Mary and Des Ward, Elizabeth and Dick Wood-Martin, and Frances and Edward Wylie-Warren.

CONTENTS

PART III: In Mediaeval Times

PART IV: After the Reformation

PART V: The Eighteenth Century

PART VI: The Early Nineteenth Century

PART VII: The Famine and the Later Nineteenth Century

PART VIII: The first half of the Twentieth Century

PART IX: Modern Times

Round Tower, Church & Celtic Cross at Drumcliffe - The Lawrence Collection

INTRODUCTION

When I told my Dublin friends that I was writing a history of my own Parish, they sympathised. I think they imagined I had a dry and dull task. Little did they realise how fascinating a project it has been. For Drumcliffe is no ordinary parish. Quite apart from the lovely scenery including mountains, lakes, woods and a glorious coastline with sandy beaches - I counted ten golden beaches, nine lakes and two lagoons - there is an absolute wealth, almost a super-abundance, of both historic and prehistoric interest.

There are at least 209 ringforts and 45 or more other pre-historic sites. The ornithology and geology of the area are exceptionally rich and interesting. There are at least twelve saints associated with the parish, seven of them actually born in it, and it has its own mediaeval martyr. There are eight castles, three of them still standing; six battles, nine or more writers, three of them born in the parish; plenty of artists; two monastic settlements, two abbeys, remnants of four high crosses, four caves, four islands, four holy wells, three Spanish Armada wrecks, and many differing legends!

The area of Drumcliffe parish is wide. I include Rosses Point which for most of its history has been part of Drumcliffe Parish, and Ahamlish which came in with Drumcliffe in the eighteenth century, and Lissadell which for a period became a separate parish and later was re-united.

No one writes about history without a bias of some sort; but although I write as a member of the Church of Ireland, I have tried within that parameter to be as unbiassed as possible.

I have tried to interweave a rather broad background picture of the history of Ireland with the narrower focus of the history of the parish; and include something of local colour and social history as well; and at the same time to explain the traditions that lie behind the story of Drumcliffe monastic settlement; and then later try to simplify for newcomers the strange workings of the Church of Ireland. I have also tried to keep it readable in spite of this ambitious goal. The text is divided into sections rather than longer chapters, and this should I hope make it easier to skip should you wish to do so - but try and read it all, you'll learn something new I hope. May you enjoy reading it as much as I enjoyed writing it!

Stella Durand, Lisnalurg House, Sligo.

DRUMCLIFFE - The Church of Ireland Parish in its North Sligo Setting.

i

PART I: NORTH SLIGO

ORIGIN OF THE NAME

When we start to investigate the origin of the name Drumcliffe, we are soon led back to ancient history. The name 'Drumcliffe' is an anglicisation of the Irish *'Druim Cliabh'*. Joyce and other dictionaries of place-names only fairly helpfully translate this as 'Ridge of the baskets'. The meaning has been disputed, and 'the ridge at the back' is also given (the back of the mountain). However the basket meaning is nearer the mark, as 'cliabh' undoubtedly means wickerwork stakes. *The Dinnseanchus*, a rather fanciful ancient book explaining place-names, talks of a fleet of one hundred and fifty wickerwork curraghs being prepared there by Curnan Cos-Dubh (the black-legged) "a man of valour beyond poetic praise" in order to besiege Ainle, son of Lughaide (Leo) of the Long hands, at Dun na mBarc. (1)

This fort was a nearby settlement in the area of Magherow, or possibly Moneygold suggested antiquarian Henry Morris.(2) Magherow was a generalised name for the whole peninsula in ancient times. Morris points out that the Book of Lecan calls Dun na mBarc 'the territory of the cairns' and 'Cairns' is an older name for Moneygold, where there are indeed the remains of a large cashel with ten foot thick walls and a souterrain, and with a suitable natural harbour nearby. Some Bronze Age artefacts from this fort are on display in the Sligo Museum in Stephen street. A stone cashel with human remains has been found recently on nearby Dernish Island.(3)

Lughaidhe(Leo) had pillaged Drumcliffe, but by the time the fleet of boats was ready he had died, and his son Ainle was the recipient of Curnan's revenge. Curnan is said to have worked on the boats for a year and a half in secret, making them from wickerwork and stretched hides. He continued the siege for a year and a half, and finally killed Ainle, his queen and all his family. The village of Carney possibly got its name from Curnan, the Irish being O'Carney's land.

A more prosaic explanation of the name Drumcliffe could be that plenty of hazel was growing there which was particularly useful for making the sturdy ridges of baskets and also very likely the wattles out of which the houses were made long ago- the strong hazel upright stakes between which the lighter willows were woven. Thus the name would more correctly be something like "wattle stakes" or "wickerwork stakes"! Woodmartin mentions (4) that in his day (1882) the area was known for wickerwork, and basketwork has continued to be made in the village until very recently, willows still being abundant. Another explanation offered by O'Rourke is that the place was studded with the wickerwork cells of monks and thus it got its name.(5)

Only in modern times has the river become known as the Drumcliffe river - although Bord Failte calls the river the Cowney. It had several former

DRUMCLIFFE - The Church of Ireland Parish in its North Sligo Setting.

1

names. *The Book of Fenagh* calls it(6) the Lainne, after Mog Lainne an ancient chieftain who was the only person to die during the battle of Cooldrevny- of which more later. He died by disobeying orders and crossing the Druid's 'erbe' (it is not known exactly what this was, possibly a fence or magical boundary of some kind) according to one source, and crossing the river according to another. Certainly Knocklane is Hill of Lainne (*cnoc lainne* in Irish), and an island on Glencar Lake was Inis na-Lainne. Other ancient names for Drumcliffe were Cnoc na Teagh - possibly Hill of the House, and 'Drumderg (red hill) of the Fenians' (*Agallamh na Senorach - Colloquy of the Ancients*).

BENBULBEN

Drumcliffe lies within the Barony of Carbury, also known as Carbury of the Battles. The piece of land betwen Benbulben and the sea was obviously ideal for blocking the progress of any army descending from the north. The written history of Carbury goes right back to the fifth century although the boundaries of it have since changed slightly. It is named after Cairbre, the third of the eight sons of Niall of the Nine Hostages, Prince of Connaught and High King of Ireland. The dominant landmark in it is the imposing range of mountains culminating in the peak of Benbulben, 1,722 feet above sea-level. The slopes are grassed up to the start of the limestone cliffs, and then the heather moors spread all along the flattish top, with many little lakes and pot holes, making it very dangerous for hillwalkers.

The etymology of Benbulben is again disputed; either 'hill of the hawk', or 'peak of Gulban'. Conall Gulban was another son of Niall, who was fostered near it by his uncle Brian who settled at Glencar. As there were many Conalls he took the name of the nearby mountain as an extra nickname to distinguish him. He was an ancestor of the northern O'Neills. Truskmore further along the Dartry range has a Telefis Eireann transmitting station on its summit, and signs of prehistoric habitation have been discovered on its slopes. The peak of Ben Whiskin on the northern side is an unusual shape, and near here is the horse-shoe valley or Gleniff, with its triple cavern, one of them magnificently vaulted, on the hillside which has associations with Diarmid of legendary fame. During the Civil War hostilities when the Irish Republican Army were digging a trench they found an ancient burial-place on the side of Benbulben with an urn and an old weapon, which are thought by archaeologists to be even earlier than Diarmid.

The beautiful waterfall at Glencar features in Yeats's poem "The Stolen Child". Yeats used to say that at certain times a huge door would open in the face of Benbulben to allow the faery hosts (the 'Sidhe', pronounced 'shee') to spread over Connaught.

THE LEGEND OF DIARMID

The story is that Diarmid hunted, killed, and was mortally wounded by an enchanted wild boar. While he lay wounded, his enemy Finn took such a long time to fetch him some water that he expired before it reached him, and he was

DRUMCLIFFE - The Church of Ireland Parish in its North Sligo Setting.

2

buried beneath the brow of the mountain. Diarmid's father had killed someone's favourite hound, and in retaliation a curse had been put on Diarmid that if he hunted a wild boar he and the boar would have the same life-span. There are spots on the mountain now called variously 'Dermot's bed', 'The Swine's Grave', and 'Finn's Seat'. Diarmid and Grainne his bride had eloped from the palace at Tara, and legend has it that the dolmens scattered around Ireland are Diarmid and Grainne's beds, that he erected for her to shelter under on their flight from their enemies and to happiness and marriage in Sligo. They lived at Rath Grania near Collooney.

PREHISTORIC REMAINS

There is a very wide variety of pre-historic remains in the area, with New Stone Age, Bronze Age and Iron Age all represented. There are plentiful ringforts, souterrains, bronze age wedge tombs, fulachta fiadhs, and court tombs. We find also a portal dolmen, stone cashels, middens, promontory forts, a fine hill-fort, an ogham stone, barrows, cairns, mounds, ritual enclosures, sweat-houses and moated sites.

In 1935 the Fourth Harvard Archaeological Expedition, led by Hencken, excavated the Court Chamber tomb with its two-chambered gallery at Creevykeel just north of Cliffoney.(7) It is one of the finest examples of a court tomb in Ireland, and is dated circa 2,500 B.C., the beginning of the Bronze Age. Chips of cremated bone were found there and also pottery, axes and a stone bead. In more modern times it has been used as a drying kiln for flax, and as a poteen still, before excavation. The circular cashel called Cashelbawn, up the hill above Cashelgarron, has twelve foot thick walls; Cashelgarron cashel itself, nearer the main road, is largely in a broken condition. Killsellagh wedge gallery grave was discovered by members of the Sligo Field Club in 1963. There are court tombs also at Castlegal, Streedagh and Cloghboley, and nearby a fine one at Magheranrush or the Deerpark, and remains of one at Mount Temple.

These and the portal dolmens are thought to have been places of ritual and tombs for cremated remains, some of which have been found there. Near Ballintrillick on the north side of Benbulben there was a fine portal dolmen in the townland of Clough. Unfortunately the enormous stones of this "Druid's Altar" as it used to be called in the old days, fell down the hill when sand was taken from the spot for the construction of a road for the television transmitting-station at Truskmore in 1961. Cist burials have been found in a number of places in the parish.

On the river bank opposite the site of the Old Rectory there are remains of a Bronze Age Wedge Tomb surrounded by cairn of stones and standing stones, including a cist burial place. There are a number of Bronze Age burial places throughout the parish. A simulation of part of a stone circle has been erected in the new St. Molaise's park in the centre of Grange village. A large stone, possibly with ogham writing, is lying in a hedge in the townland of Derry. Still a mystery is the site high on Benbulben's southern slope, where there is the ankle-high

DRUMCLIFFE - The Church of Ireland Parish in its North Sligo Setting.

3

square foundation of some building; a hermitage has been suggested, also that it may date from the Mediaeval period.

There are remains of two crannogs (lake-dwellings on artificial islands) visible at the west and east ends of Glencar Lake, and a pair of decorated early Bronze Age axes found on one of these is now in the British Museum in London. After drainage, four other crannogs were visible at the west end of the lake, built on a base of radiating beams. These were homesteads of the O'Rourkes until comparatively recently, probably up to the sixteenth century. There are two fulachta fiadhs, or communal cooking-places, at Finned near the shore, and at Lower Rosses. There are moated sites at Rahelly and Collinsford.

Clough Portal Dolmen near Ballintrillick - Drawn by John Arthur Wynne, 1838

FORTS

Earthwork ringforts - generally called raths - which were fortified farm-steads from the Iron Age, are dotted all over the parish. It is interesting to speculate if these green mounds with their souterrains were the places where the Firbolgs and Tuatha de Danaan retired after the invasion of the Milesian Celts, giving rise to the legend of the "little people". 'Lios', 'rath' and 'dun' are inter-changeable terms for earth forts; stone forts tend to be called cashels.

Four larger forts, at Lissadell, Lisnalurg and Rathbraughan, are particu-larly interesting. Lisnalurg, which is one of the largest in Ireland, is now thought by archaeologists to be Neolithic, the larger one a ritual enclosure. The fosse or ditch surrounding the central mound is thought to have been filled with water, giving the appearance of a crannog. The smaller lios on the townland has the unusual feature of a rectangular banked enclosure adjacent to the mound.

DRUMCLIFFE - The Church of Ireland Parish in its North Sligo Setting.

4

IRISH LAKE DWELLING OF THE ISOLATED TYPE.
Ideally restored from inspection of numerous sites.

Lissadell fort has a crypt or chamber beneath the central mound, and it was inhabited as late as the thirteenth century. Rathbraughan is very large, an excellent example of a multivallate (with several surrounding banks) hill-fort.

There are three or four circular stone cashels in the parish, and three of them - Inishmurray, Cashelbreen and Cashelbawn with its twelve foot thick walls- are on a line with each other, and also on a line with the earliest rays of the sun at the winter solstice(8). The dun at Doonfore incorporates a more recent stronghold of the O'Harts. There is an Iron Age promontory fort called Dun Farach - or sometimes Dun Feich - on the sea side of Knocklane hill, and within it can still be seen a very small part of the ruin of a small mock-castle built there by the Gethins, the landlords, as a sea-side cottage and tea-house for picnics. All that remains now is part of a wall, also part of the look-out post on top of the hill. Dun Balra, a fort almost buried in sand near Ahamlish, has long been associated with Balor, a Fomorian chief, also known as 'Balor of the evil eye' - very much the 'bogeyman' of folklore. His wife Kathleen apparently fought valiantly by his side in every battle. Besides Dun Farach there are three other promontory forts in the area, two on Mullaghmore headland, and one on Inishmurray.

INISHMURRAY

This is the gem of the county. The name means island of Muredach, and Muredach appears to have been the first Abbot, under the authority of the Prior of Aughris. The monastic remains here are surrounded by what is possibly a more ancient cashel or fort, as there is evidence of human occupation from pre-historic times. The chapels and beehive huts, are in very good condition; there are several other buildings of great interest, and carved crosses. Some good books have been written about the island, notably by Dr. Patrick Heraughty and by Joe McGowan, and these are invaluable guides to the island's mysteries. Just to whet one's appetite there are the old cursing stones and a sweat house among other

DRUMCLIFFE - The Church of Ireland Parish in its North Sligo Setting.

5

things, and six sleeping chambers within the cashel walls - probably essential to withstand the Atlantic winds in winter.

A legend about the cursing stones says that they can never be counted; and the idea of them is that you do the stations widdershins or anti-clockwise and turn them over as you say your curse, but if the curse is unjustified, it falls on your own head; alternatively you can turn them sunwise or clockwise if you want to bless someone. Some of the stones are carved, the most elaborate example being the one in the Duke of Northumberland's museum annexe at Alnwick Castle in the town of Alnwick in Northumberland in the north of England. (10) I found it well-displayed on a recent visit.

The panel with five crosses has been adopted by Sligo Cathedral as an official "Sligo Cross". The crosses are taken to represent the five wounds of Christ. The monastery was raided by the Vikings in 795, and burned by them in 806, but the monks continued on until at least the twelfth century, with a shore base Abbey at Staad or Staid near Streedagh on the mainland. There was always a king of the island, and the Heraughty and Waters families have both had this honour in the past. An eighteenth century traveller, Gabriel Beranger, visited it in 1779 and found no priest, doctor or lawyer there, but said the islanders were healthy, naturally religious and never quarrelled!(9) Knowledge of herbal cures was of course more extensive then, and they were more commonly used.

The crozier and bell from the monastery are also on display at Alnwick Castle Northumberland, in the small museum in the courtyard, and were probably acquired along with the cursing stone and other items by the Duke of Northumberland some time post 1836, purchased by his agent from Roger Walker of Rathcarrick House near Strandhill - a friend of Petrie's, and an avid collector of antiquities.(10) Decorated croziers were usually reliquaries, containing remains of a saint's original staff. The plain wooden staff of St. Molaise shows through, in fact, where the outer case is damaged. The island can only be reached in fair weather and boats go out there in summer from Mullaghmore and Rosses Point. In the eighteenth century the men of Inishmurray would pilot boats into Sligo harbour. The island was inhabited until 1948, and the purest Irish was said to be spoken there. In 1948 the inhabitants were re-housed at Milk Harbour in the townland of Mount Temple near Ahamlish.

ST. MOLAISE

The local saint associated with Inishmurray is its sixth century abbot, St. Molaise, also known as St. Laisren. Laisren was a common name then, meaning, some scholars suggest, a leper, as all skin diseases tended to be lumped together under that title in those days. The biographer of St. Molaise of Leighlin explains (11) that Molaise was a pet-name for Laisren, (Mo [= my], Lais[ren]) and suggests that Laisren (also Laserian) is a form of the Gaelic 'Lassair' meaning 'flame'. There are records of seven or eight St. Molaises from Ireland's Golden Age of saints. Molaise of Inishmurray (son of Declan) and Molaise of Devenish (son of

DRUMCLIFFE - The Church of Ireland Parish in its North Sligo Setting.

6

Naitfraech) and Molaise of Leighlin (son of Cairell) are the best known.

Father Dennis Molaise Meehan of the Meehan family of Ballaghameehan near Rossinver who are traditional coarbs of St. Molaise, suggests that the Devenish and Inishmurray saints could possibly be identical, having lived in the same era(12). The tradition on the island has been that this is so. However it is unlikely, as St. Columba had St. Molaise of Inishmurray as his confessor, whose dates would indicate that he was older than St. Columba. Whereas the younger saint would not seem a likely choice, as his known date of birth would show he was only seventeen at the time of the Battle of the Books.

The full-size oak statue of St. Molaise (about five feet four inches tall) is on exhibition at the new National Museum extension at Collins Barracks in Dublin. It is beautiful workmanship, thought to be from around the late Thirteenth or early Fourteenth Century on the basis of the garments. The face of the saint has an aura of holiness about it. The back of the statue has been hollowed out, it is thought in penal times, with the idea of providing a boat to escape in case of need. There are various local stories about the statue, and magical powers are attributed to it. The *Protestant Penny Journal* called it the figure-head from a wrecked ship; and unfortunately the hands are broken off. There have been many attempts to destroy the statue by misguided Protestants, by burning, drowning and shooting at it out at sea, some say by the Sodens, but these attempts all failed, and the statue is reputed to have miraculously returned to its niche unharmed. In the late nineteenth century it was painted red.(13)

Statue of St.Molaise
by kind permission of the
National Museum of Ireland

DRUMCLIFFE - The Church of Ireland Parish in its North Sligo Setting.

7

The old manuscript Gospel of Molaise no longer exists - burnt, Fr. Meehan claims, by one of the twelfth century Meehans to put an end to the quarrelling over who should possess it! But its shrine was used for many years by local judges in preference to the Bible to get the truth out of people. It is richly decorated and is on display at the National Museum in Dublin. The Teach Molaise on the island is one of the oldest stone-roofed buildings in Ireland. A red lichen grows there which is locally known as "St. Molaise's Blood". St. Dicuil (Latin version: Dicolla) was the Abbot in the eighth century, dying in 747.

SLIGO

The name Sligo, meaning 'shelly', is amply justified in the parish, with deposits of oysters, clams, periwinkles and cockle shells found on the raised beaches at Carney and Ballincar. But the appropriateness is completely fortuitous as the name is pre-Gaelic and applied first to the river, as did many other pre-Gaelic names, which would have been kept by the invading Celts out of respect because they were all associated with gods and goddesses.(14)

The parish has a beautiful stretch of coastland, from Bowmore Strand at the Rosses, to Drumcliffe Bay which is anciently known as "Culcinne's strand" round to Lissadell beach and the Yellow Strand past Raughley to the fossil rocks and spectacular sandhills and lagoon of Streedagh, to Milk Harbour and Dernish Island and the attractive fishing village of Mullaghmore with its blue flag beach, Bunduff Strand. Mullaghmore is dominated by the Scottish baronial-type castle of Classiebawn , built by Lord Palmerston so that his daughter could improve her health in the fresh air and Atlantic breezes. Palmerston also improved the land, draining it, and raising the tenants' standard of living, and also endowing Catholic and Protestant schools alike in the area (eventually) and building a harbour and fishermens houses. See more about this further on.

TOWNLANDS

Many of the names are very interesting. Magherow is *Machair Eabha* and means the Plain of Eve, and is one of the oldest areas in the district. Similarly Drumcliffe Bay was once called 'Eabha's Strand' because there Eabha the leech-woman to Lady Cesair, the first invader of Sligo, is said by the *Dinnshenchus* (included in *The Book of Ballymote*) to have fallen asleep and drowned. The Annals record that Magherow was cleared of trees in 1102 B.C. by Fomorian settlers. Ballynagalliagh means town of the old women (meaning the nuns); Keelty means a forested place. Cashelgal nearby has the Irish name of *slieve-gan-baisted*, which means 'the mountain without baptism', which sounds interesting, but sorrow no doubt lies behind it; maybe it was rather remote and so there was no priest within calling distance if a new-born babe was dying and needed baptism. Horse-shoes are still being dug up in that townland near the peak of Lugnagall on the north side of Cope's Mountain. There exist two differing explanations. One is that in the Penal Times in the eighteenth century mounted Protestant Yeomen were riding on the slopes there, searching for Roman Catholics who were holding illegal masses, and a guide led them to a cliff and they all fell over. The other version is similar, but the horsemen were Cromwell's army and their commanding officer Sir Frederick Hamilton, and they were lost in a mist. The spot is dubbed to this day "The Protestant Leap".

Breaghwy means wolf-field, Lisnalurg is fort of the hollow or fort of the tracks, Urlar a level place and Teesan a muddy place. Ballintrillick is interesting, it is marked on old maps simply as Ballagh, and its Irish name is *Ballagh na tri lig* and means the way of the three stones, from three specific flag-stones nearby in the townland of Shancrock, in front of Hollyfield School.(15) Cooldrumman the back of the ridge, Lissadell the fort of the blind man, Ballinphull the town of the hole, to name but a few. Ballincar is particularly interesting, meaning town of the pillar-stone, which refers to the stone which used to stand at Stone-Alone Point (the name corrupted today to 'Stand-Alone Point') which was at the head of a fearsat leading to *Cuil-Irra*.

Coolbeg - small back - was also called Court, and local lore is that there was a nunnery there. Magheragillananeeve means grassland of the servant of the saint; Cashelgarron is the fort of the horse, Streedagh is stripey place, Ahamlish ford of Molaise. Kintogher is interesting, it comes from the Irish *ceann tochar* and means head of the fearsat or causeway, which it in fact is. Grange too is fascinating, not least because its name is *Grainsig* which means a granary, and there was an old tithe-barn - until recently behind the present village street - which used to belong to the Cistercian monks of Boyle. Nearby is the site of the old castle - the present day school playground.

Other townlands include Castletown, which as the name suggests is the spot where a castle stood. A fragment of a thirteenth century castle can still be seen in a shady corner in a field at the junction of two roads. The Annals describe this castle as "the first cradling place of the O'Connors-Sligo, and where they grew to be powerful".(17) The O'Connors retired here after the Battle of Crich Carbury (against the O'Connells) just to the north of the parish, in 1181. They became Lords of Carbury and Sligo, then in 1536 Teigue O'Connor became The O'Connor Sligo.

Ahamlish means ford of St. Molaise. Ahamlish parish is the most northerly in the Diocese of Elphin. It was part of Drumcliffe parish in 1674 and again in the twentieth century. This is where there are the famous 'carrick spania' or Spaniards' rocks, near where the three Armada ships were wrecked on the beach at Streedagh (there is more about this further on, in the section on Elizabeth I's reign). This section of the parish contains the attractive fishing village of Mullaghmore, a popular seaside resort with a long golden beach; also the island of Inishmurray and the little harbour of Milkhaven or Milk Harbour.

Cregg means rugged rock, and the rock of the name is traditionally associated with the crowning of kings. The townland also has associations with St. Columba who is said to have performed a miracle there for a family who

DRUMCLIFFE - The Church of Ireland Parish in its North Sligo Setting.

9

Drumcliff Parish & Surrounds

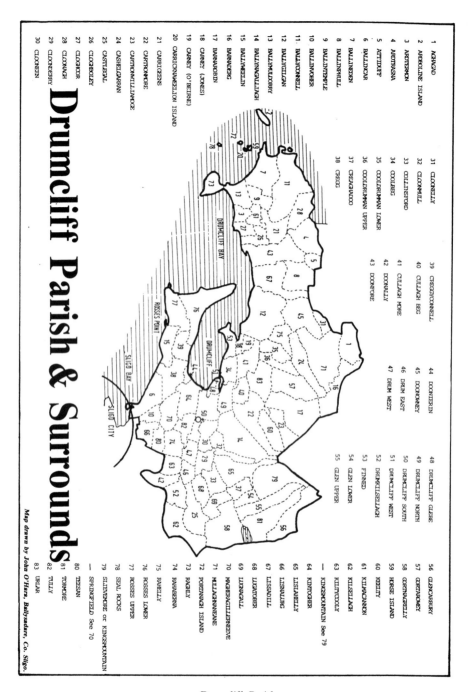

1 AGHAGAD	31 CLOONELLY	39 CREGGYCONNELL	44 DOONIERIN	48 DRUMCLIFF GLEBE	56 GLENCARBURY
2 ARDBOLINE ISLAND	32 CLOONMILL	40 CULLAGH BEG	45 DOONOMEY	49 DRUMCLIFF NORTH	57 GORTAROWEY
3 ARDTERMON	33 COLLINSFORD	41 CULLAGH MORE	46 DRUM EAST	50 DRUMCLIFF SOUTH	58 GORTNAGRELLY
4 ARDTRASNA	34 COOLBEG	47 DRUM WEST	51 DRUMCLIFF WEST	59 HORSE ISLAND
5 ATTICLIFF	35 COOLDRUMMAN LOWER		52 DRUMCILSELLAGH	60 KEELTY
6 BALLINCAR	36 COOLDRUMMAN UPPER		53 FINNED	61 KILMACANNON
7 BALLINDEN	37 CREAGWADOO		54 GLEN LOWER	62 KILSELLAGH
8 BALLINPHULL	38 CREGG		55 GLEN UPPER	63 KILTYCOOLY
9 BALLINTEMPLE				— KINGSMOUNTAIN See 79
10 BALLINROCHER				64 KINTOGHER
11. BALLYCONNELL				65 LISLAHELLY
12 BALLYGILGAN				66 LISNALURG
13 BALLYMULLDORRY				67 LISSADILL
14 BALLYNAGALLIAGH				68 LUGATOBER
15 BALLYNVELIN				69 LURGACALL
16 BARNADERG				70 MAGHERAGILLEREEVE
17 BARNAROBIN				71 MULLAGHNANEANE
18 CARNEY (JONES)				72 PORTINAGH ISLAND
19 CARNEY (O'BEIRNE)				73 RAGHLY
20 CARRICKNAWEELION ISLAND				74 RAHABERNA
21 CARRIGEENS				75 RAHELLY
22 CARTRONMORE				76 ROSSES LOWER
23 CARTRONWILLIAMOGE				77 ROSSES UPPER
24 CASHELGARRAN				78 SEAL ROCKS
25 CASTLEGAL				79 SLIEVEMORE or KINGSMOUNTAIN
26 CLOGHBOLEY				— SPRINGFIELD See 70
27 CLOGHOR				80 TESSAN
28 CLOONAGH				81 TORMORE
29 CLOONDERRY				82 TULLY
30 CLOONEEN				83 URLAR

Map drawn by John O'Hara, Ballysadare, Co. Sligo.

Drumcliffe Parish

DRUMCLIFFE - The Church of Ireland Parish in its North Sligo Setting.

offered him hospitality. Near here the Wynne family had a thatched house called "Bath Lodge" for use when bathing in the sea. (18) Also on the shore of Ballincar nearer to the town of Sligo is 'Lady Anne's Bathing Place', a shelter for her to dress in after swimming. Lady Anne was the wife of John Arthur Wynne, nee Lady Anne Butler, who died in 1840.

FOLKLORE

As well as having a wealth of ancient history and mythology, the area also has its share of folklore. One is charmed by the magical sound of the legend of Finn MacCool freeing Benbulben of its monster, and the tale of the waterhorse. The story is that this waterhorse from Glenade Lake chased and killed a woman who was hanging up her washing. Her husband killed the companion water-horse, chasing it as far as Cashelgarron, and it is now supposed to be buried in the cashel, which means fort of the horse.

A folk expression I have always liked is to call the wild days of April "the borrowing days" (weather borrowed from March); and also the term the 'Cuckoo Storm' to describe the Spring tides that bring in the wrack - the seaweed that farmers used to spread on the land to fertilize it. St. Brigid's well in Cliffoney has a story about it that St. Brigid while visiting a nearby monastery used to spend the night immersed in its water, praying and weeping; but she was spared this penance after a while by the waters magically disappearing each night, but reappearing in the morning. It is a place where people used to bury unbaptised babies. (See more about this well in the section on holy wells).

CUSTOMS

In Glencar there was a local tradition of cake-dancing. A huge cake twenty inches in diameter was decorated with flowers and awarded to the best and most enduring dancer at the end of an evening of dancing. It is still considered unlucky to bring whins (gorse) or May into the house. People would always exit by the same door they had entered or else it was considered that they took the luck of the house out with them.

Customs that still persist from the old days include the adorning of holy wells with rags as a token of thanks for a healing, the visiting of saints wells on their holy day, the burning of bonfires on Midsummers eve, the Wren Boys visiting on St. Stephen's Day, and Garland Sunday masses at the holy well sites go back to Penal Times, when people would each add a stone to a pile of stones and leave flowers. The holy wells had been sacred and also used for healing in the time before the coming of Christianity and were taken over by the Christians and used for baptisms. The 'Patterns' at the Holy Wells with their set prescribed prayers are another ancient custom that has been Christianised, and no doubt there are others.

A sad local legend is that the souls of unbaptised children, who were buried at Keelty church, would turn into owls; and the owls were well protected there. Babies who died suddenly were said to be taken by the fairies. A late nineteenth-century traveller describes a surprising local custom of cutting the turf on the top of Benbulben and then throwing it over the edge to roll down the slopes, to save their donkeys.(16) A mid-nineteenth century custom was gathering on a Sunday to drink *scolteen*, which was a beverage made from whisky, eggs, sugar, butter, carraway seeds and beer.

LOCAL STORIES

Farmers may tell one, if one is lucky, of the banshee and the fairies they have seen. There are legends associated too with the roaring hole inland from Raughley, a deep chasm called the Derk of Knocklane where the waters boil and seethe in stormy weather. Once Letitia Gore (née Booth) wife of Nathaniel Gore of Ardtermon Castle is said to have forced her coachman at pistol point to drive her round the edge of the chasm. She was said to have always dressed in white, and had her horses shod with gold. She is now called the Banshee Bawn and is believed to haunt the place!

A legend attaches to the court chamber tomb at Creevykeel, near the village of Cliffoney. The tomb, before its excavation, had been used as a useful hiding place for an illicit poteen still. The story is that one day fifty men on horseback arrived to capture the still and its owners; but the owners were warned in time by the appearance of a white hare, which led them to a spot from which they could see the horsemen arriving

An even more modern piece of folklore is that the steep Tully Hill at Rathcormack is the scene of Constance Gore-Booth driving her horse tandem over it at full speed, which gained her a strong reputation as a horsewoman in the district. This is not at all unlikely, for when her grandfather Sir Robert Gore-Booth kept the Sligo hounds, he held annual hunt races at Tully Hill, and his son could well have continued this tradition.

HOLY WELLS

There are several holy wells in the parish. St. Columba's Well is in the townland of Kintogher in Lower Rosses, and is reputed to have powers of healing, especially if used around the time of the saint's death, the 9th of June. There are also St. Patrick's Well and St. Brigid's Well mentioned above, and St. Molaise's Wells near Ahamlish church, and in Cloonagh. St. Brigid's Well near Cliffoney has a swastika engraved on the stone as part of a larger cross.

The swastika is thought by some scholars to be a pagan symbol used by early Christians as a disguised cross in

Sketch of stone at
St.Brigid's Well, Cliffoney
From J.R.S.A.I. 1880
by W.F.Wakeman

times of persecution; it has been found as a Christian symbol in third century Roman cemeteries, and on fourth century monuments. However it was also the ancient Indian symbol adopted by worshippers of Mitra or Mithras, a religion which was brought to the West with the Roman armies.(17) The swastika could have been introduced here by a youth from Roman Britain who had been captured as a slave, as St. Patrick had been.

WILDFLOWERS

The area is also noteworthy for its excellent wildflowers. The Benbulben range is particularly good, with the protected valley in a cleft known as the Swiss Valley above Glencar, and the horseshoe valley of Gleniff, and other locations as well. Here Alpine and Arctic flowers grow, such as clustered alpine saxifrage, and other saxifrages, the very rare chickweed-leaved willowherb, mountain avens, maidenhair fern, yellow poppy and fringed sandwort. (18)

The headland at Streedagh is of interest, with moisture-loving plants living in a dry habitat, bog pimpernel, sea-pink and sheeps fescue and many common orchids in early summer.(19) Ardtarmon is also interesting ecologically, with acid and alkaline plants growing in close proximity to each other.(20) Dead Man's Point at Rosses is good for sea-plants. The Yellow Strand and Mullaghmore are specially good locations for machair-type vegetation, and are rich in orchids, thyme and ladies' tresses.(21) On Inishmurray are found purple loosestrife, sea-spurry, tormentil and other potentillas, bird's foot trefoil (which is the original shamrock, *seamrog* in Irish, although we tend to use *trifolium dubium*, a small yellow-flowered clover which is actually a much later introduction to Ireland), water-avens, royal and adder's tongue ferns, allseed, lesser marshwort, germander speedwell and various bedstraws to name but a few.(22)

Along the banks beside the road there is in summer a profusion of ox-eye daisies, bush-vetch, buttercups, and also meadow-sweet (healing for arthritis); and in the damper places a lot of horsetail, a plant rich in silica which would be used far more if people realised its health-giving properties. (A case of the doctrine of signatures holding good, as the stem of the plant uncannily resembles a spine). Ubiquitous common plants include self-heal, silverweed, willowherb, pineapple mayweed, vetch, and harebells near the sea, plentiful in Knocklane. Other healing plants which are abundant include elderberries, hawthorn, dandelion, angelica and yarrow. Traditionally seaweed and nettles have also been eaten in this area for hundreds of years. Carrageen, dulse, sloke and laver are edible seaweeds; and serrated wrack - *fucus serratus* - applied externally is excellent for arthritis, and is used in seaweed baths; some local people also swear by channelled wrack, - *pelvetia canaliculata* - locally known as 'famluc'(23); but many of the seaweeds are mucilaginous.

THREE LOCAL ODDITIES

A spectacular sight along the valley towards the lake of Glencar, and so just within the borders of the parish, is the Waterflight, or *'Sruth-in-aghaidh-an-aird'*, literally 'the stream against the height', a waterfall which appears to flow upwards or at least spectacularly cascade up into the air. This happens best when the wind is blowing stiffly from the south. In the correct conditions, with freezing temperatures it has been seen to be frozen in mid-air, like delicate lacework.

Another local oddity is a seabog at Ballyconnell strand. At low tide the men of the village used in the old days to bring their donkeys and carts and their 'slans' (traditional turf-cutting spades) down to the strand and dig for turf below the high-tide-line. The turf was claimed to be Sligo's best.

A third oddity is the so-called 'Magnetic Hill' at Gleniff, part of the beautiful drive around the Horseshoe Valley there. As long as you are driving down the hill, if you stop at the sign and turn off your engine and your brakes, your car will go back up the hill! It works best for larger cars, and also for people more susceptible to optical illusions!

ROSSES POINT

The name, *Ros Ceite*, means the peninsula of the fair or market. There was great excitement here and much controversy when archaeologists Burchell and Reid Moir claimed to have found Mousterian period implements in the cave at Rosses Point and on nearby Coney Island, which they took to indicate that Ireland was inhabited by Palaeolithic man.(24) The debate continued on for a couple of years, when it was then taken out of the hands of the archaeologists and given to the geologists, with the result that in 1930 Burchell and Moir reported that the stones were not manmade implements as previously suggested but just natural pieces of rock.

The channel between the mainland and Oyster island is called the "channel of a thousand currents", with reason. The 'perches' marking the channel for cargo ships used to have lights at the top, which were trimmed and filled each day and lit each night by hand.(25) The Sligo Militia used to practice with their cannons which were kept on the headland between the two beaches of Bowmore Strand, shooting out across the incoming waves(26). That spot was also where the Rosses Point Coastguards used to signal with mirrors to the Raughley Coastguards.(27)

Dead Man's Point is so-called because a sailor died as his ship was entering port, in 1899, and the crew buried him there in a hurry, so as not to miss the tide, with a loaf of bread as they were not sure if he was really dead. The two islands across the channel are Oyster island and Coney island. They are in the parish of Killaspugbrone, near Strandhill. Killaspugbrone Church is a ruin now, but was associated with Bishop Browne a friend of St. Patrick. The New York Coney Island was named by a Rosses Point man who was captain of the ship *Arethusa* which used to sail between Sligo and New York. Washington Lodge

DRUMCLIFFE - The Church of Ireland Parish in its North Sligo Setting.

14

nearby in Ballyweelin is believed to have a tunnel connecting it with the shore, as also does Elsinore, which was used for smuggling purposes.

WILDLIFE AND BIRDS

Wildlife is good too, with foxes, hares, rabbits, field-mice, fallow deer, red squirrels, pygmy shrews, stoats, mink (not indigenous but released from farms) and badgers; and grey seals off Inishmurray.(28) There are ten species of butterflies, including small blue and dark green fritillaries at The Yellow Strand. (29) There is a good fishing lake at Glencar, well stocked with brown trout, and salmon run up the four mile long Drumcliffe River from February onwards, and are mostly caught in drag nets at the estuary. There are abundant mackerel in the bays. The rare barnacle geese and brent geese visit the area round Drumcliffe estuary from Greenland every winter, particularly the townland of Ballygilgan with its 'bruchs' - fields that are flooded in winter, and where most of the geese over winter- one of them is known locally as 'the goose field'. Lissadell is also noted for woodcock and pheasant. Ornithologists have spotted linnets, and corncrakes are being recorded and Birdwatch Ireland notified. Peregrine falcons, merlins and choughs are being noted in the Benbulben range, especially in the Swiss valley.(30) There have been no eagles since 1880.

There are eiderduck, barnacle geese and a colony of shags at Inishmurray, and also fulmars, teal, storm petrel, dunlins, kittiwakes, turnstones, linnets, wheatears, skylarks, arctic terns and more. There is a large cormorant colony on Ardboline Island and Horse Island, (which incidentally used to be known as Inishbeollain after the coarbs of Drumcliffe(31) with great black-backed gulls, herring gulls and the odd black guillemot.(32) Bunduff Lake at Mullaghmore, a lagoon formed by the damming of the Bunduff River behind the sand-dunes, has both whooper and mute swans, lapwing, teal, plover and white-fronted geese.

FEARSATS

Another interesting feature of Drumcliffe's past were the *fearsats* across the bay at low tide. These were fords or causeways. Sligo's strands have changed a lot over the years so that nothing remains of these fearsats now. One of them is said to have been used by O'Donnell on his way to raid O'Connor at Sligo, although some sources locate the fearsat used by O'Donnell at Collinsford - originally Colles' Ford - now Collinsford Bridge. This ford was guarded for O'Donnell by a rather cruel man called Colles who demanded passes from people before he let them over, or otherwise beheaded them. The only person he let off without a pass was a simple idiot who produced a playing card - an ace of hearts! Colles is also reputed to have kept a gallows on his land, on which to hang people of the 'wrong' political persuasion.

O'Donnell probably crossed at Ballincar, as the Fearsat called *Reanna an Liagin* meant Ford of the Pillar-Stone, and ran anciently from Stand-Alone Point to Finisklin in Cuil Irra. In 1928 a man recalled this fearsat and said that sea-weed

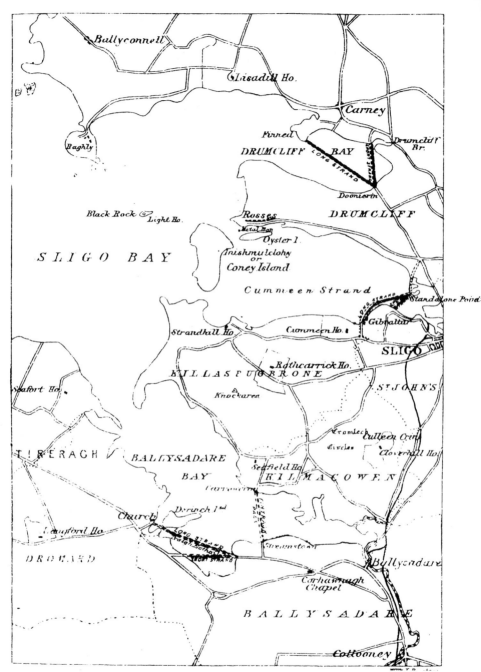

Map showing Fearsats over the bays - by kind permission of Sligo County Library

would be carted over the fearsat to Cummeen and Gibraltar, and added that the area was different then. Other fearsats ran from the edge of Drumcliffe Bay at Kintogher across the sands at low tide to Drumcliffe, to Finned and to Johnsport. The Drumcliffe one is marked on Sir William Petty's 1655 map and on the Ordnance Survey map of 1837. These causeways were often built up with bushes, seaweed, stones, timber or anything else available. Even as late as the mid-nineteenth century, boats returning to Lower Rosses with sea-weed had to wait for the tide to get high enough so that they could cross the ridge of the fearsat at Johnsport.(33)

GEOLOGY

Geologically the area is extremely interesting. The entire mountain of Benbulben is composed of carboniferous limestone, the rock having formerly been at the bottom of the ocean, and being made out of tiny shells and skeletons of marine animals, just as coral is. A good place to observe this is in the limestone shaft of a former high cross at the corner of the lane leading to Drumcliffe church. The limestone of the mountain has formed into caves in several places, and those conducting the earlier Geological Survey at the end of the nineteenth century reported that there were stone benches in the cave they called Temple Patrick, now known as Teampull Setric, beyond the waterfall of Glencar.(34) The surveyors supposed that religious meetings had been held there, but local tradition is that it was a priest's hiding place, and the masses were held at a local mass rock nearby. (35)

There are a series of small sea-caves known as The Pigeon-Holes or The Punch Bowls, near Raughley Head. There is also the small cave where the hatchet was discovered during the Civil War, on the face of Benbulben bluff, and three other 'caves', two of which are souterrains, on the Lissadell promontory. The souterrain in the mound near Lissadell Church is supposed to connect with the old O'Hart Castle at Doonfore down the road, and certainly it does extend a long way , and there is a smaller souterrain in the moated site at Rahelly, and the natural cave is further north, near Lislary townland.(36)

The most exciting local cave is on the hillside on the north side of Benbulben, near Ballintrillick, approached by the Gleniff Horseshoe Valley. It can be reached by a reasonably easy climb up the east-facing slope and consists of three caverns, one of them with almost cathedral-like vaulting.

The rocks at Streedagh Point, between the two beaches, represent the most complete section of the north-west carboniferous limestone exposed, with caninoid fossil corals. The rocks at Serpent Rock near Ballyconnell abound in fossils; there is the snake-like *Zaphrentis cylindrica* and various types of brachiopods such as *productus* and *spirifer*. There are trace fossils on the Mullaghmore cliffs, grazing trails and burrows. The rocks at Lower Rosses are pink and white feldspar, with quartzose schists and coarser gneiss, iron, some garnets and tourmalines. This is a very ancient geological era, with Archaean rocks, the oldest known.

DRUMCLIFFE - The Church of Ireland Parish in its North Sligo Setting.

—— 17 ——

BARYTES MINING

Ireland is one of the oldest barytes producing countries in the world, and there have been eight separate attempts to make a success of mining it at Benbulben.(37) Barytes is sulphate of Barium (BaSO4). In addition to its well-known use in X-rays, it is used in lead, putty, sugar, the paint industry and the manufacture of oil-cloth, linoleum, rubber, wall-paper, china, glass, asbestos and as a pottery-glaze.

Sir Richard Griffiths first identified the barytes ore deposits on Benbulben in the early nineteenth century. The first of the eight attempts to mine it was in 1859 when a Mr. Williams started a small open-cast mine at Glencar, carrying the mineral down the mountain into Gleniff on the backs of donkeys. Then from 1870 to 1879 Mr. Barton mined it; he had a thousand foot long aerial ropeway to carry the ore in buckets. It was then ground at the mouth of the River Bunduff and shipped from Mullaghmore Harbour. From 1890 for four years George Tottenham tried it, then from 1895 to 1911 Sir Henry Gore-Booth. From 1911 to 1922 The Gleniff Barytes Company extracted the ore through a tunnel.

The most interesting effort to mine the barytes from the point of view of industrial archaeology is the attempt between 1928 and 1931 by Barium Consolidated Ltd., because they constructed seven miles of 24 inch gauge railway, from Gleniff (where the ore had been purified and milled) to Mullaghmore Harbour. They had 18 inch gauge tracks along which to push containers of the ore at the top of the mountain, and a cable for the area in between the two. Benbulben Barytes mined it for the longest period of time, from 1940 to 1960; then the most recent enterprise was the American company Sligo Bay Barytes, who mined it for three years from 1976 to 1979.

The old Barytes Mill is now being restored by F.A.S. as a tourist attraction.

PART II: THE EARLY CHRISTIAN PERIOD.

COMING OF CHRISTIANITY

As far as we know, Christianity first came to Drumcliffe itself in the sixth century, though Inishmurray's monastic foundation was older than this. St. Patrick had preached in Sligo in the fifth century if our dating is right, but we do also know that there was Christianity in Ireland before St. Patrick's mission in 432. He seems to have concentrated more on the north, the west and the midlands than the south and the east, which probably reflects the distribution of Christian churches at the time. St. Columba in the mid-sixth century had travelled all around this area preaching and founding groups of Christian converts. The founding of an actual monastery at Drumcliffe was probably later again, in 574 or 575 after Columba had returned from Iona to attend the convention at Druimceatt, near Limavaddy. See the section on the founding of the monastery for more details. The old church at Keelty, below King's Mountain, now ruined, is supposed to have been founded by St. Columba as well; it is known as St. Mudhnat's church. A stone from it, with a simple Celtic cross carved in

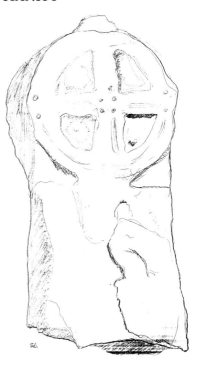

Sketch of The Keelty Slab by Stella Durand

it; the ninth or tenth century "Keelty Slab", is in the National Museum in Dublin, but not on display at present.

BATTLES

At least six battles were fought in the parish. There was a Battle at Magherow in "Anno Mundi 3656" according to the Annals of the Four Masters, which would be 105 B.C. Two very famous battles were fought in this general area in the sixth century. The first was the Battle of Sligo in 537. This was basically a rebellion of the Ulstermen and other princes against Eoghan Bel the King of Connaught. Owen died on the shores of the shelly river (the Sligeach, now known as the Garavogue). He is supposed - according to two different accounts - to have had his head cut off and carried across the plain of Magherow, and to have been buried standing upright with his spear in his hand defiantly facing Ulster at Rathveeragh. The Deerpark court chamber tomb at Magheranrush is

DRUMCLIFFE - The Church of Ireland Parish in its North Sligo Setting.

19

thought by some authorities to be his burial place.(1) The second battle was in 561, the Battle of the Books, covered in detail in the next section.

In 1051 there was a 'battle' at Knocklane, the O'Rourkes invading the O'Harts' territory. There tended to be much relocating of cattle in these small battles. In the twelfth century there was a battle between Geoffrey O'Donnell, prince of Tyrconnell (fighting side by side - at first - with his allies the O'Neills) and Maurice Fitzgerald the English Lord Justice. It was called the Battle of Credan Cille, and took place between Drumcliffe and the sea. The place name is unknown today, but it has been suggested that as Credran means a little shrine, it could have been the area of Springfield, where there used to be a stone with an imprint of Columba's knees on it. (2) O'Donnell and O'Neill defeated Fitzgerald at Credan Cille, but then as O'Donnell lay dying of his wounds he had himself carried on his bier to reanimate his troops to repel an invasion of his own lands by O'Neill.

THE BATTLE OF THE BOOKS

In 561 an important battle involving St. Columba (otherwise known by his nickname Colmcille, 'dove of the church' or church-pigeon) was fought in the parish. The reasons for this battle were complex. Traditionally every school child knows that the Battle of Cuildreimhe (pronounced Cool-drevny; but Cooldrummin is an equally correct name for the townland) is also called "The Battle of the Books".

The explanation is interesting. St. Columba was staying at Dromin or Drumfin monastery in Ulster, a monastery of his former teacher, St. Finian of Moville. St. Finian had just returned there from Rome, bringing back with him a wonderful copy of the Psalms, a better translation than had been hitherto available, with interesting glosses and liturgical rubrics and even reflections in the margin.(3) Naturally Columba wanted a copy of this for his own monasteries, for books were only come by in those days by painstakingly copying them out. So he stayed up late at night for days on end copying out the Psalter in the church at Drumfin. He was caught in the act and Finian demanded the copy for himself. Columba understandably felt he had the right to it; so they decided to bring the matter to the High King of Ireland to decide. Diarmid MacCerbail, the High King at Tara, gave the now famous verdict "To every cow its calf, and every book its copy", (the founding of the first copyright law!).

Now Columba had other grievances against King Dairmid. The High-King had indulged in polygamy, and had employed an arch-druid (Fraechan or Briochan) as his adviser instead of a Christian abbot or bishop, although he was officially a Christian; and he had violated sanctuary on two occasions, one involving the merciless killing of the son of the King of Connaught, who had inadvertently caused the death of another player while playing hurling. The Brehon Law in force at the time esteemed the concept of sanctuary very highly, and Curnan the young prince guilty of manslaughter had run to Columba for

DRUMCLIFFE - The Church of Ireland Parish in its North Sligo Setting.

—————— 20 ——————

sanctuary, as the person of an Abbott was held to be sanctuary. There were of course also territorial grievances and family feuds between Columba's own princely clan of the northern O'Neills and Dermot's, the southern O'Neills, over the High Kingship. So the relatives were summoned, and Columba's monks rallied round, and the King of Connaught supplied armies as well, so that Columba's forces totalled 2,300 "men".

THE CATHACH

I put "men" in inverted commas in the last sentence, for it must be pointed out that at that time of history women were used to fighting as well. It was St. Adamnan (also known as St. Eunan) a seventh century successor of Columba as Abbot of Iona, and Columba's biographer, who was instrumental in getting the "Law of Innocents" drafted. He achieved this at the Council of Birr in 696, and this law was passed at the Synod of Tara in 697, releasing women, children and monks from the legal obligation to fight. The law is also known as the *Cain Adamnan*.(4)

The victory went to Columba. The copy of the Psalter was then awarded to him and was in the possession of the O'Donnell family and their mascot in battle - called "The Battler"(the 'Cathach') - for many centuries. It was given by Sir Richard O'Donnell to the Royal Irish Academy in Dawson Street, Dublin. Its decorated shrine is in the National Museum. A mural of the battle of the books painted in 1948 by Sligo artist Bernard MacDonagh can be seen in Sligo Public Library which is housed in a former Congregational Church in Stephen Street.

SEQUEL TO THE BATTLE

The legend goes that Columba was so upset at the three thousand dead on the battle field that he resolved to become a missionary to Scotland to convert an equal number of pagans to the Christian faith as the number of Christians who had died that day in battle. The actual unfolding of those events was along those lines, but a little more complicated. Involved in all this was Saint Molaise of Inishmurray. Molaise was first present at the Synod of Telltown where the case was discussed by Columba's fellow-Abbots and the Bishops of the church. Here Columba narrowly avoided excommunication, thanks to St. Brendan of Birr speaking up for him, and the verdict was given that Columba should win over to the Christian faith a number of Pictish pagans equal to the number of Christians slaughtered during the battle.

Molaise confirmed this verdict when he met Columba personally at "the Cross of Ahamlish", and added as a penance the severe extra clause that Columba should be exiled from the land he loved so much. After a year of preparation spent at his main monastery of Derry, Columba with twelve monks set out for Scotland, landing eventually on the small island of Iou or Hy, later named Iona, which the King of Dalriada had given him. This small island was the focus for a major missionary effort to convert the Picts which also spread to the North of England.

FOUNDING OF DRUMCLIFFE MONASTERY

St. Columba returned to Ireland on three more occasions, and it was on one of those visits that he is thought to have founded the monastery at Drumcliffe in 575, 14 years after the battle. Columba had sworn that as part of his exile he would never set eyes on Erin again, or set foot on her soil; legend has it that when he returned he did so blindfolded and with Scottish turves strapped to his feet.

There is no actual proof that he founded Drumcliffe monastery, but the strong likelihood is there, as it is mentioned as a Columban foundation in two separate Monasticons, and so was definitely part of his *paruchia* or family of monasteries. *The Book of Lismore* and the *Life of St. Farannan* both assert that he founded a religious house in Carbury after the Convention of Druimceatt. And we know too the circumstances of his having the land. It is reported in two places(5) that it was given to him by his friend and kinsman Aedh son of Columba's uncle Ainmire, both of whom later became High Kings of Ireland. Aedh's gift was prompted by the fact that his daughter drowned in a pool on the Drumcliffe river and God restored her to life through the prayers of Columba, so Aedh gave the land to God and to Columba for ever. Columba in turn bequeathed the headship and succession to the clan O'Connell for ever, and we see a succession of O'Connells in charge all through the Middle Ages. The successor to the abbot was known as the *coarb*, and the Drumcliffe coarbs were always known as 'coarbs of St. Columba'.

St. Columba was fond of Drumcliffe as we see from a fragment of a poem attributed to him:

> *"Beloved to my heart also in the west*
> *Drumcliffe, at Culcinne's strand."*

St. Columba was a member of the *fili*, the ancient Irish Order of Poets and Bards, and he saved this Order from being disbanded when he returned for the Convention of Druimceatt in 575 (at Daisy Hill near Limavaddy). He also achieved a greater measure of independence for Dalriada (later, with Pictland, to be renamed Scotland), from its overlords in Erin. Columba, with his princely O'Neill blood, was ever a great negotiator with Kings and we can easily imagine this tall man with his restless energy and his mane of red hair (his baptismal name was Crimthann, the fox) and his grey eyes and beautiful singing voice, as what he might have been, a High King of Ireland.

All we know about this early foundation was that he left Mothorian or Thorian- now St. Mothorian - behind as its abbot and he also left it equipped with a bell and a chalice. Mothorian is described in the *Martyrology of Donegal* as "holy, radiant", and he is honoured on the 9th. of July. Columba himself is honoured on the 9th. of June. *The Book of Lismore* also adds that Columba left the newly founded monastery with a crozier made by himself, and this is not at all unlikely, for these early Christian abbots often had skills that would be useful in their monasteries; Columba was also as we know an accomplished and very fast scribe. A Columban monastery continued on in the spot for almost a thousand years longer, the last known abbot dying in 1503.

There are some traditions about this early church. One was that it was always called The Yellow Church, or Templeboy (*teampull buí* in Irish). This could be because of the thatch, and there was a thatched roof to the church at Drumcliffe right up to the mid-eighteenth century. The other tradition was that it had a college or monastic school attached which was of far reaching influence with foreigners attending it. In the old Annals, Drumcliffe is sometimes called "Drumcliffe of the Crosses"; this could be because in 871 one of the Lords of Carbury, Dunadhachm , "a famous man by whom hostages were held" died and was buried "under hazel crosses at Drumcliffe."(6) The hazel had been considered sacred by the ancient Irish. Or it could refer to the four or more carved stone crosses.

PROBABLE LAYOUT OF THE MONASTERY

The first monastery would have consisted of a wooden church, and a group of wattle and clay round-houses or cells, all within a triple bank with ditches between. The slightly later stage of development of this particular settle-ment would, archaeologist Joyce Enright reckons, have been at least 22 acres in area, and would have included several mills as well as churches and houses and monastic cells, the college, and a souterrain;(7) (this was unearthed when the road was widened). As time went on stone buildings would have been erected, and by the tenth and early eleventh century there was the round tower and the fine Celtic Crosses, one of which now stands near the entrance to the roadway to the church. The old sixteenth century map by Sir William Petty is one of several which show two churches in Drumcliffe, for the men and women perhaps, as on Inishmurray.

It is open to debate whether there was a stone church, or stone churches, in the monastic period, and if so did it stand on the site now occupied by the nineteenth century church, or nearer the Round Tower. The door of the church is aligned with the door of the round tower. Some scholars think that the tower is too distant from that site for it to be the site of the original church also, but eighteenth century writers have stated that the church of that time was on the site of the Abbey. Gravedigger Bertie Monds when digging Yeats's Grave which is close beside the church, found several large foundation stones.There were no monastic but rather secular remains to be found in the excavations to build the car park. However both opinions are mere conjecture.

Round Tower at Drumcliffe - The Lawrence Collection

THE ROUND TOWER

The tower is thought to have been built circa 1,000 A.D. It would have had many functions. One of them is obvious from an old name for a Round Tower, namely *cloighteach* or bell-house, a place from which to ring the hand bell. It would also have acted as watch tower and also a defence in case of attack by the Vikings - or by local raiders from rival clans, as plundering was a favourite occupation of Irish chieftains! This explains why the doorway is high up, so that the ladder could be brought in and greater safety ensured. However the monks had not thought of the danger of fire, and scholars tell us that the round towers tragically made excellent chimneys. Another ancient name for the towers is *cloch anchore*, house of the anchorite.(8)

Another purpose was for storage, and sometimes too there would be a scriptorium in the room at the top. The towers would also have been useful landmarks as most of Ireland was still forested at that time. The tower at Drumcliffe was damaged by lightning in 1396, the wall being badly cracked in three places. In 1739 the Revd William Henry reported that there was a wide chasm in between the two halves. When antiquarian George Petrie visited it in 1818 he sketched it and one can see from his sketch that it was a lot taller then and there were also several cottages attached to its base.(9) In the mid-nineteenth century a road contractor blew up the tower to loosen the stones, which he then used to build the bridge over the Drumcliffe river. Local legend has always been that the tower will fall down when the wisest man in the world passes under it.

THE HIGH CROSS

This is the only complete Celtic Cross standing in Co. Sligo. The design is a very fine one, and scholars have seen similar designs occurring around 1100, called the Urnes style, which helped to date this cross as approximately late eleventh or early twelfth century.(10) It is happily in a fairly good state of preservation as its sandstone has a high proportion of quartz in it and is hard-textured and difficult to cut, so it has resisted weathering fairly well, although concern about it is now being expressed. The very top portion is missing. This was a small carving of one of the wooden churches, a *dairtech* or oak-house, with overlapping round wooden roof tiles. A drawing by William Jones who accompanied the Welsh antiquary Edward Lhuyd to see the cross in 1699 and 1700, shows it with its little church-shaped top in place.(11)

Dr. Harbison has conjectured that the top and shaft may not have been originally designed to be together, as the bead-work has had to be narrowed to match up the top and bottom and there is an empty space near the join.

The circle which is such a distinctive mark of the Celtic Cross has been interpreted in several ways: some see it merely as a functional item to support the structure, others see it as a symbolic expression of the integration of sun-worship with the Christian religion; others prefer to see it as the cross embracing the whole world,

Drumcliffe High Cross
Courtesy of the O.P.W.

and everybody in it, and being larger than the world and at the centre of creation. Others see it as the halo of holiness surrounding the head of Christ. However the idea of combining the empty cross with the victor's wreath was fairly widespread in the Roman Empire from the fourth century onwards. Very ancient too is the idea that the heavy base represented the hill of Calvary. What is certain is that the carvings on these crosses were originally painted in bright colours, and were a type of strip-cartoon of Bible stories to serve an educational purpose, much as stained glass did in the Mediaeval times. They were preaching stations too, with people gathering round to be told the stories depicted on them.

The front, or east face of the cross at Drumcliffe has pictures in relief of Adam and Eve, Daniel in the lions' den, a camel and Cain killing Abel with a spade; the west face has the presentation of Christ in the temple (or possibly the judgement of Solomon), an Irish wolfhound, the arrest of Christ in Gethsemane, the crucifixion with a lance and sponge, and two figures, possibly John with a scroll and Mary with a veil, or else the two thieves. There are various animals on the narrower north and south sides, including a rather nice frog, a seal and a stag crouching; there is also a Mother and Child figure on the south side, and of course many of the intricate spirals for which Celtic art is famous, symbolising eternal life.

OTHER MONASTIC REMAINS

The tall limestone shaft at the corner as one enters the lane leading to the Church is now known for certain to be the shaft of another high cross. Dr. Peter Harbison has found a picture of the cross dated around 1780, in the Cooper Collection in the National Library, soon to be published in his forthcoming book, which shows it with its head in place. There is also a mortise hole at the top where the head of the cross would normally have been joined on to the shaft. The gravedigger, the father of Bertie Monds, said to his son years ago that there were heads of several crosses to be found in the graveyard. This is borne out by the Revd William Henry who stated in 1739 that there were several large stone crosses there and some of them were half buried in the ground. (12)

Three broken segments of a third fine carved cross are in the National Museum in Dublin. They had been 'bought' by a collector of antiquities, the lawyer Roger Walker of Rathcarrick near Strandhill Co. Sligo, for the sum of fifteen shillings, as noted in his account book, in August 1837 - the sum he paid for a pair of boots for his wife Amy or two boxes of rusks for his children, and slightly cheaper than his annual subscription to the Law Library! (13) After a period when they were in Sligo Abbey they went to the National Museum in Kildare Street. There are two fragments of the shaft, and part of the head. The east face has a carving of a man killing a lion, the sacrifice of Isaac, and Daniel in the lion's den; and the west face has the Resurrection and the mocking of Christ.

There was also a stone known as "the angel stone", with an unusual carving, presumed to represent the Angel which legend says led Columba's

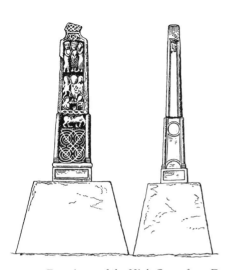
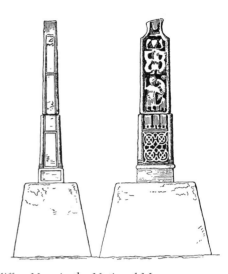

Drawings of the High Cross from Drumcliffe - Now in the National Museum

High Cross Upper Stone
by kind permission of
Martin A. Timoney

soldiers into battle on the day of the Battle of the Books. This is not to be found at present, but a fairly similar carving was for many years incorporated into the boundary wall of the Round Tower in a horizontal position, beside the stile. The stile has now been replaced by a gate, and the carved stone has been removed to the workshops of Duchas in Dromohaire for restoration. It is thought by archaeologist Martin Timoney to be possibly the base of another High Cross. Half buried in the graveyard Joyce Enright discovered a single early Christian cross-slab similar to the ones abounding on Inishmurray.

Two fragments of a probable fourth high cross were discovered during repairs to the church in 1999 in preparation for the opening of the Visitor Centre, when the plaster was removed. They are both incorporated into the inner walls of the church, one on the left in the porch and one on the right inside the church on the west wall. These are of sandstone and have intricate geometrical designs carved on them, and possibly a figure of some kind, but the stone is

High Cross Lower Stone by kind permission of Martin A. Timoney

too worn to be certain. Research into them continues, with the present preferred date between the 8th. and 10th. centuries. We are probably looking at the sides of a cross shaft, with a very broad width - the sixth broadest in Ireland, according to Martin Timoney who has researched them extensively.(14) The large hole at the base could be, he suggests, where relics were placed, with a little wooden lid.

OTHER CHURCHES

Apart from the three monasteries already mentioned - Drumcliffe, Inishmurray and Staad Abbey - there were at least seven other churches known about in the parish, and one of them, Ballynagalliagh, was a convent. Ballynagalliagh means town of the nuns and was also locally known as "Nunstown". The nunnery there became a daughter house of the Augustinian Convent at Kilcreevanty near Tuam in Co. Galway around 1223.(15) They were Augustinians of the reformed or Arroasian Observance- vegetarians, wearing white clothes and observing strict silence. The Kilcreevanty foundation appears to have been well-endowed, owning five quarters of land in Sligo. The Ballynagalliagh nuns were well-provided for, because the tithes of Drumcliffe in mediaeval times before the Reformation were divided in four equal parts, the bishop's, the nuns', Lord Clanricard's and the rector's.

The old farmhouse there has been traditionally understood to be a remain of the nunnery, possibly the hospital, which was known to exist in 1427. (16) Three sides of it are red sandstone and only the front is limestone. Within living memory there was an old washing place of the nuns in a hollow nearby, locally called "The Soap House". It had stone flags on the floor, and was surrounded by interlocking stones. According to Bertie Monds who was reared near the spot, and who ploughed that field, the nuns used to take in washing to earn their living, and there is a smell of the soap still in the soil, after four hundred years!

St. Mudhnat's Church at Keelty, below the mountain, was another old church in the parish, and a small ruin can still be seen. There was at least one ancient church at Rosses. There are no remains, but the old graveyard can still be seen beyond the golf links. The old stone church at Ballintemple has substantial ruins still, and is enclosed by its small disused graveyard, and with an old stone millstone lying outside the walls. A few fields away is the beautiful cross-inscribed slab or pillar stone, which is similar to those on Inishmurray but also unique in design as far as we know. These stones were used as boundary markers and grave markers and battle markers from earliest times, and were Christianized by the addition of the crosses to them. Ballintemple in Irish is *Teampull Beollain*, and is another sign of the O'Beollains' presence in the area in mediaeval times, along with Ardboline and Inishboline islands.

There are very slight remains of a church at Derrylehan. The old stone church in Church Hill Wood on Lissadell Demesne has only very slight remains, but the second Lissadell Church was at Bun Breunoige, and was probably a wooden chapel built after the Penal Laws were relaxed, but already ruined by 1837. There is also an old grave-yard at Carrigeens.

Sketch of Ballintemple Cross-Slab by Stella Durand

The Keeloges church, although a ruin, is in good condition, and has a fine pointed stone arch. It is reputed to have been founded by St. Molaise. There is also a curious stone head there, at present part of the gate-post, which is very ancient, and is locally believed to be able to cure toothache if one touches it when affected.

OTHER SAINTS CONNECTED WITH DRUMCLIFFE

Another saint who is mentioned in connection with Drumcliffe is St. Patrick, although his connection with the area is extremely slight. The Tripartite Life tells us (19) that he walked through Rosses and Drumcliabh on his way to build a church at Domnach mor Mauge Ene, somewhere near Ballyshannon and Bundoran. On his way he is said to have cursed the Duff river and blessed the Drowse - still a good salmon river to this day !

Three female saints were associated with Glen Dallan, the old name for Glencarbury, the western end of Glencar, the Co. Sligo part. They were the three sisters of St. Molaise of Devenish on Lough Erne, daughters of Naitfrech, their mother was Monoa or Monua; all three are commemorated on January 6th. The first sister Tullala went to Kildare and became abbess of St. Brigid's convent there. Osnata founded the church of Killasnet, named after her, which is at the eastern end of Glencar, in Manorhamilton Parish Co. Leitrim. Muadhnata (St. Mudhnat) lived at 'Caille', which is an obsolete name now, but some presume because of the similarity of the names that she founded the nunnery of Ballinagalliagh which later became affiliated to the Augustinian House of Kilcreevanty, but 'Caille' could equally well be Keelty (*Coillte* in Irish), which is where her church is. Then there was St. Dallan himself, father of St. Loman of Lough Gill, the hermit who was contemporary with St. Columba, and lived on an island on the lake, and is reputed to be buried on Church Island, possibly in the stone lined grave near the church. St. Loman assisted at the Synod of Druimceatt, welcoming St. Columba from Scotland. St. Dicuil was another Inishmurray saint, Abbot there in the seventh century. His feast day is 27th.October.

The first Bishop of Elphin, left in charge by St. Patrick, was St. Assicus. He was a royal bishop and also a worker in metal who made chalices and quadrangular patens and bookshrines for Patrick, and is said to have founded a school of metalwork in Roscommon. From this school came the craftsmen who made the beautiful Ardagh Chalice and the Cross of Cong, two of Ireland's greatest treasures. Assicus was known for penance and austerity, and spent many years doing penance as a hermit (for shame because of a lie told about him) near Slieve League cliffs, Co. Donegal. He is buried at Racoon Hill near Ballintra and his feast day is 14th. April.(20) Then St.Torannan, the tenth century Abbot of Drumcliffe who died in 921, was considered its patron saint for many years. He was described in the Martyrology of Donegal as "lasting, deedful, over a wide shipful sea."(21)

LIFE IN A COLUMBAN MONASTERY

The monks were considered to be soldiers of Christ and so lived a very ascetic life, eating only twice a day, and mostly porridge or bread and vegetables. They worked hard, prayed hard and studied hard. Work could have been farming, fishing or copying out books, and worship happened at regular hours throughout the day, with an emphasis on the Psalms, all 150 of which they aimed to memorize. The distinctive mark of Irish Monasticism was that it was both cenobitical and eremitical - that is with monks who were both living in community and hermits each having his own cell. There would also be periods when they withdrew to a wilder place on their own for periods of deeper prayer and penance.

This monastic type was modelled very much on the monasticism of the Egyptian desert, whose influence came to them from St. Martin of Tours their chief inspirer, and through him from John Cassian. Travelling around and sharing their Christian faith with others and so founding new churches was one of their main occupations, and serving the communities they lived amongst with teaching and healing. Their lives were simple, harsh and yet joyful. The combination of the hermit's life with the community life seemed to breed monks who were loving and harmonious among themselves, quarrels were not a feature of their lives - miracles were. No one told them that miracles didn't happen today, and they took the Bible seriously, and in simple faith expected miracles to happen, and so they did.

They also each had their soul friend, their *anamchara*, to whom they would make their confession, and their practice of this is considered to have introduced the Sacrament of Penance as a feature of the Pre-Reformation Church.

Even the abbot would have his soul-friend. They wore plain unbleached woollen robes and only the abbot wore a white cowl as a badge of office. Their hair was tonsured in the druidical fashion from ear to ear, the front half of the head shaved and the back half hanging long.

Drumcliffe Church in winter

DRUMCLIFFE - The Church of Ireland Parish in its North Sligo Setting.

31

PART III: IN MEDIAEVAL TIMES

DRUMCLIFFE IN EARLY MEDIAEVAL TIMES

Drumcliffe was an important place from the sixth until the twelfth century, an Episcopal See, and often mentioned in the Annals. That it was large is testified to by the fact that it was said to have twelve hundred wooden houses built of ashwood. It was thought in its heyday to have been a settlement of some ten thousand people. If you wanted to indicate a large amount of Ireland, you often said something like "all the way from Kells to Drumcliffe".(1) Armies often passed by carrying their plunder, for it was the main gateway between Ulster, then called Uladh, ('Ster' is a Danish suffix), and Connaught.

In 830 the Vikings came to Connaught leaving wholesale destruction in their wake. They sacked churches and burned houses, and whole villages, and had no respect for the church. In 950 an important death is recorded in the Annals, of Flann ua Becain, Erenach of Drumcliffe, son of the abbot, a learned scribe.(2) Fourteen years later there is the record of the death of Muirenn, a female erenach,(3) and earlier in 934 "Uallach, poetess of Ireland".(4)

Unfortunately no records survive telling us when the Diocese of Drumcliffe became united with Elphin, but the probabilities are in 1111 at the Synod of Usneach, or in 1152 during the complete reorganisation that happened then following the Synod of Kells, or in 1224 which is when the See of Ardcarne was united with that of Elphin. Under the auspices of St. Malachy there were radical reforms and reorganisations in the twelfth century, and at the Synod of Kells the present diocesan system was created, with thirty-six dioceses within four provinces or archdioceses. The archbishopric of the east was moved from Glendalough to Dublin, so as to include the Danes or 'Ostmen'. The four provinces were Armagh, Dublin, Cashel and Connaught (later renamed Tuam). Drumcliffe, when it was a see, would have been in the province of Connaught. Elphin would then have been regarded as the more senior diocese because it had been founded by St. Patrick. But we do know that in 1152 Elphin was reckoned to be one of the richest sees in the country.

EXTRACTS FROM THE ANNALS

In 1018 the Annals report that "The Hairy Star" was seen for a whole fortnight, around harvest time.(5) This one assumes to have been a comet. In 1029 there was a tragedy when 62 people were burnt to death on an island called Inis-na-Lainne, (which is thought to have been the western crannog on Glencar Lake - the source of the river Mog Lainne - hence Inish(island)Lainne). The Erenach of Drumcliffe Aenghus Ua hAenghusa perished there. He had met up in conference with the Lords of Carbury and Dartry.

The other people burnt there would have been their respective retinues, probably having rowed to their destination in curraghs, suggests O'Rourke. Fires

DRUMCLIFFE - The Church of Ireland Parish in its North Sligo Setting.

32

on islands and especially monasteries seemed to be a feature of the Middle Ages. Another very tragic fire nearby was in 1416 when the O'Cuirnan library went up in flames on Church Island in Lough Gill. This was said to be the finest library in the west, and many precious documents and manuscripts must have been lost to us in this way, including, tragically, two books the *Screaptia O'Cuirnin* and the *Leabhar Gearr*, which were said to rival the *Book of Kells*.(6) The lost *Book of Sligo* could very well also have been among the manuscripts lost in this way. The O'Cuirnans were hereditary scribes and genealogists to the O'Rourke family.

In 1091 a great snow is recorded, which killed people, cattle and birds; but later that year it turned out to be a 'sappy plentiful year' of good weather.(7) We gain so much from reading between the lines, not difficult in the following entry:"1128: a one and a half years' peace between the men of Connaught and the men of Munster"!(8) Then in 1133 "a great cow disease was after coming to all of Erinn, for which no likeness was found for 432 years."(9)

THE COMING OF THE NORMANS

Soon after this, in 1168, the Anglo-Normans were invited into Ireland by Dermot McMurrough King of Leinster. This provided the opportunity to instigate what had already been planned between Pope Adrian IV and King Henry II of England. The face of Ireland changed from a collection of monastic settlements and towns and villages grouped around them, to a more urban culture, with the great Norman castles as the central pivot and smaller castles too, all acting as manors. The first great spate of stone church building was begun, and there might have been a stone church in Drumcliffe at this time. We cannot be certain. It was in this century that the O'Connors settled in Carbury, from then on in constant competition with the O'Donnells for supremacy over the area.

From the accounts in the Annals we gather that Drumcliffe was still an important place, and features quite often in the exploits of princes. It was still common practice then for aristocrats and royalty to join monasteries, as it had been since Patrick's day. The new Bishop of Elphin, Florentin MacRiagan O'Mulroney, was a descendant of the kings of Connaught. He was also a Cistercian monk and formerly abbot of Boyle; he died in 1195.

In 1225 the death is recorded in the Annals of Auliffe O'Beollain, Erenach of Drumcliffe, described as a wise, pious and learned man, known for his generous hospitality; he was also a *betagh*.(10) A *betagh* was a kind of public victualler, a man whose job it was to offer food and hospitality to people, and he had land for that purpose, usually around 480 acres. Betaghs held this land free of rent but in return had to entertain travellers and the chief's soldiers. Auliffe could well have died of the 'heavy burning sickness' which was decimating the population of the towns that year.

In 1245 there was a new bishop, John, but the circumstances of his consecration proved difficult, as although the Pope had agreed, the Archbishop of Tuam wanted to acknowledge English royal supremacy over Ireland, so he

DRUMCLIFFE - The Church of Ireland Parish in its North Sligo Setting.

33

waited until the next year for royal assent. (Erastianism before its time!) And all for very little, as Bishop John only lasted less than a year. This was the year in which Maurice Fitzgerald built a castle in Sligo, in present day Castle street, the scene of many violent raids, and finally destroyed in 1595, demolished by the then owner, O'Donnell, for fear the English might inhabit it.(11)

RIVAL BISHOPS

In 1260 the Bishop of Elphin since 1247, Thomas O'Connor, was elevated to be Archbishop of Tuam. It is interesting to see that he consecrated the Dominican Abbey at Roscommon newly founded by Phelim O'Connor. His translation was the signal for chaos to begin and for two years there were two Bishops in the Diocese! Although Milo MacThady O'Connor was consecrated at Dundalk by the Archbishop of Armagh, and had the necessary royal approval, the cathedral officeholders all regarded his elevation as irregular. The Dean, the Archdeacon, the Treasurer and the Provost of Elphin together presented Thomas MacDermot to the King protesting the irregularity of Milo's election.

Their case was supported by the Archbishop of Tuam, who, receiving Royal approval, proceeded to consecrate Thomas. But Milo had no intention of relinquishing his appointment. So Thomas then appealed to both the Pope and the King, and obtained at last a writ from the King that Thomas should 'have the temporalities' i.e. enjoy the tithes and live in the palace and receive stipends and rents. Milo conveniently died at this juncture, which saved him the public mortification of being officially displaced by Thomas! The feud had continued for a space of two years.

Thomas had three years to enjoy his Bishopric, but enjoy was hardly the word, for he had a lot of trouble with Hugh O'Connor the claimant to the title King of Connaught, who coveted the episcopal revenues. This time, Thomas MacDermot appealed to King Louis IX of France (later to become St. Louis King of France) and the Queen of Castile. After his death Hugh O'Connor succeeded in usurping the revenues. The next Bishop, an abbot of Boyle - Maurice O'Connor - may have been able to regularise matters as he remained in office for eighteen years.

THE LATER MIDDLE AGES IN DRUMCLIFFE

In 1296 Malachy MacBrien became the new Bishop of Elphin. He also had trouble over obtaining his temporalities and was obstructed in this by no less a person than the Lord Deputy. He was obliged to sue.

Donat O'Flanagan was the next bishop, elected in 1303. He was one of the most competent and popular bishops yet. He was known for his hospitality and peacemaking between the people of Connaught. He was described as "full of wisdom, efficient, charitable and openhearted".(12) It is no surprise to learn from the Annals that he also died "worn out" as a result of his hard work! His successor was consecrated at Avignon in 1310 after trouble over the invalid consecration of the Abbot of Lough Ce was dealt with.

The Annals report plunderings in 1187 by the Lord of Breffni (Breffni is present day Leitrim, and the O'Rourkes were the lords of it) accompanied by many "foreigners of Meath".(13) The weather in this part of the west of Ireland has not changed much, for in 1252 there was reported a 'Great Wind on the Octave of the Epiphany',(14) which was described as prostrating several houses and churches throughout the land of Erin. In the same year one of the O'Beollain coarbs of Drumcliffe died, described by the Annals of Lough Ce as "a man of the greatest prosperity, wealth and esteem, of greatest charity, hospitality and honour of his own time in Erin, who died after the triumph of devotion and penitence".(15)

In 1278 there was a wholesale massacre of local chieftains including the O'Connors, by the McClancy clan from Leitrim. The occasion for this massacre was the assassination of the King of Connaught, Tadhg, followed by the murder of Ruairi the rightful heir on the borders of Drumcliffe. The Annals add that 'the swarthy parson' was also killed.(16) Although the records of Drumcliffe parsons only start in 1402, we know from The Annals of Lough Ce and two other Annals that he was the son of Tigernan O'Conchobair.(17)

But although there is no mention of the character of the swarthy parson, Drumcliffe does have its very own martyr, Nicholas O'Donnchada, who as "a priest and a pure virgin" in Drumcliffe, was killed in 1306 without cause or offence by the Barretts.(18) It was accounted a martyr's death, and all who recited a Pater Noster for the good of his soul were offered one hundred and twenty days remission of their sins, for each recital!

In 1315 Drumcliffe was attacked by a woman, Dervorgilla the daughter of Murtough Muimnech O'Conor and wife of Aed O'Donnell King of Tyrconnell. She came with a band of gallowglasses (mercenary soldiers, usually heavily armed infantry) and men of the Murtagh clan, and plundered the Drumcliffe churches (note the plural) and several of the clerics and coarbs, while her husband was busily occupied in attacking Sligo Castle. On a lighter note, in 1355 the Annals of the Four Masters record that a sheep brought forth ten lambs!

OF BISHOPS AND BATTLES

In 1357 another new Bishop, Gregory, was consecrated. He was given the See of Elphin in compensation for a mistake made by the Pope. He had already been consecrated at Avignon as Bishop of Down, the former Bishop of Down being believed to be dead; but to everyone's embarrassment the Bishop of Down turned out to be very much alive!

In 1416 Maurice O'Connell was burned in his house by 'reavers' (a band of plunderers). He was a *coarb*, which means literally successor, for all the monastic offices were hereditary under Brehon law, and even laymen could inherit them, if they were chiefs, but they usually took minor orders in such a case.

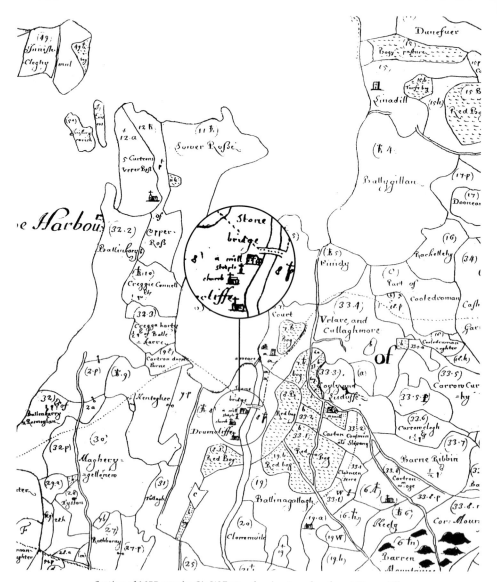

Section of 1655 map by Sir W.Petty, showing two churches at Drumcliffe
by kind permission of Trinity College Dublin Map Library

In 1444 the Bishop, William O'Etegan, and many of the Connaught clergy went to Rome on a pilgrimage, and the Bishop died there. In 1495 there was another small battle in Drumcliffe this time between two of the opposing O'Connor claimants to the succession, with the help of many other local families. Felim O'Connor was the victor.

ORGANISATION OF THE MONASTERY UNDER BREHON LAW

We do not know the exact date when the monastery came to an end. The record of the erenachs and hereditary abbots show that the last recorded death of an abbot, one of the O'Beollans (Bolands), is in 1503.(19) The hereditary offices came down through the same two families, the O'Bolands and the O'Connells, for hundreds of years. The *coarb* was the successor of the original founder of a monastery, and usually related to him by blood ties. The coarbs could often be laymen, but they held church lands and were in charge of making sure that the Bishops received their dues.

The *Erenachs* were lower down in the hierarchy, more like land managers, though originally they had the status of Archdeacon. They too became laymen as time went by but were tonsured like the monks and so enjoyed the status of clerics - sort of paraclerics, but with taxes and tithes and land management duties. Then there were also *betaghs*, whose job of providing hospitality for the poor and also for travellers has already been mentioned; land was set aside for this purpose. Other local families at this time included the O'Harts of Grange Castle, as well as the O'Harts of Ardtarmon and Doonfore, supporters of the O'Connors.

Brehon lawyers were judges who had a long training, memorising the ancient laws probably in verse. They had also been priests in pagan days, but later the office became secular and hereditary. The laws laid a great stress on compensation and were very fair, but regarding the land they were very feudal and hierarchical. They encouraged a system of fostering children, which did have the effect of drawing people more closely together.

They also had a strong conception of sanctuary, and of honour. The people would go out to the Brehon at some spot in the open, and he would hear both civil and criminal cases. The Brehons continued on until the beginning of the seventeenth century, until after the Battle of Kinsale. Brehon Law was then outlawed by the Attorney General, Sir John Davies.

FIFTEENTH CENTURY SCANDALS

Records of the fifteenth century, the century before the Reformation, reveal a church obviously very much in need of reforming. For example one reads of a rather lazy Bishop, who resigned, thinking himself "unequal to so great a burden, from the craziness of old age and a dimness in his sight".(20) However, he was not totally crazy, as he was able to reserve an annual pension for himself of 50 marks, for his lifetime!

And for another example, there is the fascinating tale of the litigious vicars of Drumcliffe. There were in fact four men fighting over who was the rightful vicar of Drumcliffe, and one imagines that Drumcliffe then must have been a "fat living" for them to have fought over it so much!

The story begins in 1402 (21) with John O'Connell being Vicar of

Drumcliffe for a year or more without actually having been ordained as a priest yet! The next year Dermit Macherleginn was appointed vicar by the Pope under two conditions: if either John O'Connell had died or if he failed to be ordained within a year. O'Connell in fact died within the year, and so Dermit became, as he thought, the vicar.

However, Cornelius O'Connell had other ideas. He opposed Dermit and took possession of the living, appealing to the Pope. The people of the parish asked an objective observer - the Bishop of Ossory - to enquire into the matter, and this Bishop decided to absolve Cornelius of any foul play. Dermit was naturally upset by this and appealed to the Pope, who awarded the Incumbency to him in May 1405.

RIVAL VICARS LITIGATE

But the troubles were not over yet. All was quiet for twenty years, and then Nemeas O'Beollayn took Dermit to law, and Nemeas was now awarded the vicarage. He then told Dermit he could be paid a yearly sum in lieu of the incumbency. Amazingly, Nemeas received absolution for this act of bribery! Next Nemeas became Canon of Elphin Cathedral and a Prebendary of Killala Cathedral.

But all was not well, for soon both of these offices were declared illegal, and William O'Beollan, another cleric, informed the Pope that Nemeas was a fornicator, a perjurer and many other things besides, and suggesting that Nemeas be deposed and himself, William, be appointed to the office of Vicar of Drumcliffe. So William became Vicar of Drumcliffe. But Nemeas was not to be deposed. So the two rival vicars took the matter to the Abbot of Lough Ce (Lough Key) who unfortunately was himself not above taking a bribe - from William this time! A private arrangement was then reached between William and Nemeas, namely that each should receive the tithes of whichever parishioners supported them. So for some time they were BOTH vicars of Drumcliffe!

Nemeas must not have liked the work involved, as he eventually agreed that William could be the Vicar if he paid Nemeas a yearly sum. This whole scandal having begun in 1446, continued for nine years, until 1455, when Eugene O'Connell became Vicar and both William and Nemeas had their nemesis and were forced to depart. (See Appendix B for a list of all Drumcliffe's rectors, with their dates).

DRUMCLIFFE - The Church of Ireland Parish in its North Sligo Setting.

38

PART IV: AFTER THE REFORMATION.

THE REFORMATION

By the sixteenth century the Reformation was almost overdue. For example pluralism was common not just amongst the more junior clergy, but even the sixteenth century Bishops had several livings, often some in England and some in Ireland. Bishop John of Elphin, who died in 1537 even had three livings concurrently - he was abbot of Welbeck in Nottinghamshire, and Prebendary of Ampleford in Yorkshire, and also Bishop of Elphin in Co. Roscommon(1). Even after the Reformation, one Bishop was a concealed papist and he "wasted the See(2)" during his office and left it worth barely anything. Bishop John is said to have lived a concealed but died a public papist; his redeeming feature was that he was a good preacher.

Eugene or Owen O'Conogher, the Prior of Aughris, 'conformed' to the 'new religion' in 1584 and was made Dean of Achonry, Skreen, Ahamlish and Minevoriske(Drumcliffe), which were all then dependencies of Aughris.(3) The next vicar we have any firm record of since Henry VIII's Act of Supremacy in1536 bringing about the Reformation, is Thomas Pilley in 1611. So there must have been chaos and confusion for half a century, when no records were kept. Pilley was himself the holder of two livings. We must remember that in Ireland the Reformation did not take place in quite the same way that it did in other countries like Germany and England, where it had a more easily observed transition. It happened much more gradually here.

Although the law of the land now declared that the church was now "the Church of Ireland", with King Henry the Eighth as its Supreme Head, for all practical purposes everything went on as before, only gathering a bit more momentum in the short reign of his son Edward VI. There was a patchiness about the Reformation in Ireland, for some vicars had already heard about the new movement and others had not; some wanted to go along with it, others were loyal to Rome and to the Pope, and it took a long time to get it organised. The whole situation was extremely fluid.

QUEEN MARY

Although there were no major changes under King Henry VIII or Edward VI, under Queen Mary who came to the throne in 1553 there was a complete reversal for the five years of her reign. The law now declared that everyone had gone back to being Roman Catholic again. But again it was not a major upheaval. There were some burnings at the stake, but all in England - after all there had been very little reformation as yet to undo. So there was no persecution here in Ireland, although one had been planned.

The plan for persecuting Irish "Protestants" was rather cleverly foiled, the administration here playing for time, and then Mary's death at the right time

DRUMCLIFFE - The Church of Ireland Parish in its North Sligo Setting.

39

releasing them from the necessity of any persecution! (The story goes that a Liverpool landlady in an inn, who happened to be an Irish Protestant, heard her guest, Dean Cole of St. Paul's, talk of the plans and pat his pocket talking of a warrant there; so when he was asleep and snoring she substituted a pack of cards for the warrant in his pocket. This was rather embarrassing for him when he finally arrived at Dublin Castle and threw it dramatically down on the table , the joker topmost!. The Lord Lieutenant is reported to have suggested they try again in a couple of years time, and meanwhile shuffle the cards!)(3)

ELIZABETH THE FIRST'S REIGN

When Elizabeth the First became Queen of England and Ireland in 1558 she continued the policies of her halfbrother Edward, and the Church of Ireland gradually became more 'Protestant'. She soon had in place a system of fines for non-attendance at Church, forcing the Church to proceed with the Reformation. The closing down of the monasteries was one of the measures she went ahead with. From what one reads of Irish history at the time, the closing of some monasteries was no loss, but the mendicant orders seem to have been some of the very few people actually preaching the Christian gospel at the time immediately preceding the Reformation.

Queen Elizabeth appointed efficient and experienced administrators who were able to push ahead with the reforms. Unpalatable as this is to us now, the truth must be told that Adam Loftus the Archbishop of Armagh and Primate of Ireland was eager to persecute Roman Catholics, and complained that the Lords of the Pale were all of that persuasion.

Queen Elizabeth met with resistance from the native Irish aristocracy, and also had difficulties with the Spaniards. Spain had a strong link with the Irish Roman Catholic Church, and a particular interest because of her late sister Queen Mary's marriage to King Philip of Spain. The famous invincible Armada, that Spain sent, foundered very badly during storms here on the Sligo coast as well as all over the west and south coasts of England, Scotland and Ireland.

Old maps dating from 1609 mark three ships as having sunk at Streedagh beach in 1588. These are now known to have been the *Juliana*, an 860-ton ship registered in Sicily; the *Lavia*, a 728-ton ship registered in Venice; and the *Santa Maria de Vision*, a 666-ton ship registered in Ragusa, (present day Dubrovnik). Captain Francisco de Cuellar who came ashore at Streedagh, had been in command of the *Pedro*, but had transferred to another ship for a court-marshall.(5)

Three bronze guns have been recovered from the water, two of which Dúchas are preserving in water in Dromohaire. One is a pedrero, plain , and capable of firing stone shot; a second is a saker, (see the photograph) and has the inscription 'S.*Severo*' on it, and the date MDLXX - 1570 - on it, and a picture of a bishop. The bishop is probably Saint Severus himself, ('*Santo Severo*' in Italian). He was a fifth century bishop of Naples; this points to the probability of the gun being from the *Juliana*, the Sicilian ship, as Naples was part of the kingdom of

Sicily in the sixteenth century. The third gun, another pedrero, is undergoing conservation at the National Maritime Museum in Dun Laoghaire, Co. Dublin. Marine archaeologists have retrieved beautifully crafted jewellery and other treasures from the *Girona* sunk off the Antrim coast and the *Trinidad Valencera* off the Donegal coast, which indicate that the officers had a very high standard of living on board.

Sir Geoffrey Fenton visited Sligo at the time of the wrecks and reported having found eleven hundred dead men on a beach five miles long. Some of the local chieftains entertained the survivors, O'Rourke of Leitrim being one, and MacClancy of Lough Melvin another. In Ulster some thousand of the survivors under their commanding officer entered the service of O'Neill. In all, twenty-three ships are known to have been wrecked off the coasts of Connaught and Ulster.

Canon from the Juliana
Now with Duchas in Dromahaire

THE SPANISH ARMADA SURVIVOR

One of the very few documents which records the experiences of a survivor of the Armada wrecks, is a letter written by Captain Francisco de Cuellar who was wrecked off Streedagh.(6) He crawled first to Staid Abbey, (Latin statio=base, the shore base of the Inishmurray monastery), near Streedagh, which he found had been plundered and the monks hung from the iron gratings of the windows. Then he limped his way, half naked and with a bad leg to Sir Brian O'Rourke's house, probably his Glencar Crannog, as these crannogs were used as places of safety during times of attack. O'Rourke was away, but while there Cuellar heard of a Spanish rescue ship. Seventy of his companions managed to reach this ship in time, but it was wrecked and two hundred men were drowned.

Captain de Cuellar then went in search of help, living on blackberries and wild cress, and receiving kindness from a local girl who bandaged his wounds and gave him food. He was forced to work for a blacksmith for eight days, but managed to escape and find his way to Lough Melvin where he was held as a "guest" of the local chieftain McClancy at his castle at Rossclougher. McClancy treated him well, and he stayed there some time, amusing the McClancy ladies with palmistry, and holding the castle against Sir George Bingham's men, and refusing an offer of marriage to McClancy's sister. McClancy's son warned him that he was really a hostage and would probably be imprisoned, so he escaped north to Dunluce, making from there to Scotland and then to Antwerp, where he wrote the letter.

It is remarkable that we have this testimony, as it was against the law to harbour any prisoners and the local people were instructed to put to death any Spaniards they found, which seems very harsh. Sir Brian O'Rourke who also sheltered many Spaniards was hanged in London in 1591 for treason for his pains, and McClancy was killed eventually by Bingham.

Much speculation has gone on about whether or not there was intermarrying of west of Ireland women with Spanish sailors. It is often cited to account for a certain swarthiness in the west of Ireland people. This is a possibility, but we should also remember that there had been trading with Spain and North Africa there since the centuries before Christ, and recent writers have suggested(7) a large influx of North Africans in the Fourth Century A.D. - Christians from the Donatist schismatic church fleeing from persecution. This could account as well for the very early island monasteries pre-St. Patrick along the coast, together with a similarity of style in the carvings on the stones crosses to Coptic designs seen in Egypt. Having said that, the local tradition that some of the Grange families are descended from Armada sailors is very strong.

ELIZABETHAN REBELLION

During the reign of Elizabeth there was much rebellion, mostly but not all in Munster. The Pope was offering the same spiritual rewards for rebelling against the Queen as people had in former days received for going on a crusade, so the rebellion was in effect elevated to the status of a crusade, with the Pope's banner carried in battle, and the battle-cry "Papa Aboo!" As well as the Desmond in Munster, two Northerly chiefs were involved, O'Neill of Tyrone and O'Donnell of Tyrconnell.

O'Donnell had been holding Sligo Castle against Sir Richard Bingham and in 1595 he demolished it lest the English inhabit it. O'Connor Sligo was on the English side, for he was besieged in Coloony Castle, by the O'Donnells and O'Rourkes. Sir Conyers Clifford in 1599, attempted to rescue him, marching from Boyle with 2,000 men, and was routed, in the famous Battle of the Curlews. In 1600 O'Neill of Tyrone, after a short truce negotiated by Essex, joined O'Donnell. They marched with all their combined forces through Drumcliffe and across the fearsat on Drumcliffe bay on their way south to Munster, where the Spanish were landing in Kinsale. At Kinsale, in 1601, the battle turned out badly for the Spanish troops helping the native Irish and well for Elizabeth I's royalists, ending an era of looking to Spain for hope and help.

THE FIRST PLANTATION FAMILIES

With the seventeenth century, and the defeat of the two rebel Earls, the rebellions were by no means over. King James and his son King Charles had as hard a time as anyone else trying to govern the Irish. James I's solution to the problem was the idea, peaceful in theory, of Plantations - 'planting' on the land Protestant families who had served him well. These men were called 'undertakers' because they undertook to settle the land with English tenants.

There had been some plantations in Elizabeth's reign, then major ones in James's reign particularly in the North-West, and some families who planted Fermanagh and Donegal penetrated south to Sligo, among them the Gore family. Thomas Pilley was followed as Vicar of Drumcliffe by Hugo Hohy in 1615(8), and a regular succession of clergy now starts for the church in Drumcliffe which seems to have been becoming a little more settled.

THE GORE FAMILY

The Gore family who played a prominent part in local history, are traceable back to Alderman Gerard Gore of the City of London, the son of John Gore. In 1598 his eighth son, Paul Gore, came to Ireland as commander of a troop of horse, and served under Mountjoy, Queen Elizabeth's new Lord Deputy, who arrived in Ireland in 1600 with a huge army of twenty thousand men. In 1602 Gore performed a valuable political mission for Queen Elizabeth, escorting Rory O'Donnell and probably Sir Donough O'Connor to Athlone, they being the last Irish chieftains to submit after the battle of Kinsale. He was awarded a grant of land from the Queen, receiving a further grant later from King James. He was active in civil life, being the first Member of Parliament for Ballyshannon, and Justice of the Peace. He was created a baronet for his services to the crown in 1621 and is buried in the Abbey Church at Donegal town. His fourth son was Sir Francis Gore of Ardtermon.

There was a Gore castle at Coolbeg on the shore of the Drumcliffe river, dated between 1689 and 1702,(9) possibly the home of one of Sir Francis's younger sons. Its ruins feature on many maps, but there is no trace of it now. Sir Francis Gore was granted Ardtermon (pronounced Ardtarmon) Castle, near Raughley, built by the O'Harts. The O'Harts were the next most important Irish chiefs in the area after the O'Connors, and they were a family in honour of whom the blind harper O'Carolan composed some of his tunes. Doonfore Castle at Ballinfull was also built by and owned by the O'Harts and they took over Grange Castle too, which had previously belonged to the O'Connors. Other very old family names in the Grange area are Kilmartin, Crolly, Ronan, Gillan and MacSharry.

Sir Francis completely remodelled Ardtermon Castle into a semi-fortified Tudor mansion with three foot thick walls, two circular towers and a large bawn or defensive wall protecting a courtyard at the rear. The dampness of Ardtermon and the danger from stormy tides prompted his great-grandson Sir Booth Gore to build another mansion in a sheltered place by the shore at Lissadell. The date of this building is guessed to be the later 1750's, as the two full-height curved bows would place it around the mid-Eighteenth Century, and we know that the old Mass House that used to be where its stables were built, at Bun Breunoige, was dated 1746-1756 in the Ordnance Survey Letters of 1837. This attractive and unusual house, which was demolished in 1833, was at the edge of the sea halfway down what is the present front avenue.

Mid-eighteenth century house at Lissadell - Courtesy of Sir Josslyn Gore-Booth

Ardtermon Castle later burnt down by accident and was in ruins for many years and has recently been restored by the owners of the firm of Schiller and Schiller, three members of whose family are buried in Lissadell graveyard following a tragic aircrash.

Ardtarmon Castle in present day - By kind permission of Miss Bianca Schiller

People often wonder about the double barrelled surname of Gore-Booth. The following piece of potted family history should explain. Sir Francis Gore's eldest son, Sir Robert Gore Kt., lived at Newtown Manor Co. Leitrim, having inherited the property from his mother the heiress Anne Parke - see the section on the Parkes below. Sir Francis was recommended for a baronetcy in 1656 but appears not to have taken it up, for either political or financial reasons. He was succeeded by his son Nathaniel Gore who married in 1711 Lettice or Letitia Booth, (the 'Banshee Ban' mentioned in the Folklore section) the daughter of Humphrey Booth of Dublin. Their son Booth Gore was created a baronet in 1760. He was succeeded first by his eldest son also called Booth, who died unmarried in 1804 and subsequently by his younger son Robert Newcomen Gore who assumed the additional surname and arms of Booth in the same year. The Booths' substantial property in Salford, near Manchester, devolved onto Sir Booth Gore the second when his uncle died unmarried. W.B.Yeats remarked that the country people still called the family the Gores, as they disapproved of the Booths who were merchants(10) - a strange snobbery!

LISSADELL

The name Lissadell means fort of the blind man. It has associations with three poets - Muiredach O'Dalaigh, Eva Gore-Booth and William Butler Yeats. *The Annals of the Four Masters* mention a castle there in 1213 and in 1397.(11) Lissadell in the thirteenth century was the home of Irish language poet O'Dalaigh (full name *Muiredach Albanach O'Dalaigh*), a member of a family of hereditary poets and head of a school of poets. In 1213 he is recorded in the Annals as having inadvertently killed Fionn O'Brollaghan the steward and tax collector who was collecting on behalf of the landlord, the O'Donnell of the day. This happened in anger as O'Brollaghan subjected Muiredach to sustained and heavy verbal abuse. After fleeing to Mayo and then Scotland where he became famous and left behind a poetic dynasty, the poet was reinstated in O'Donnell's favour by composing a eulogy about him. On his return to Ireland he gained the extra name of 'Albananch' as Scotland was known as Alba at that time. He then entered a monastery and turned his skills to religious poetry.(12) Even in translation his lines are beautiful. On the death of his wife he wrote:
> "My soul parted from me yestere'en
> A fair form that was dear to me lay in the grave...."(13)

Lissadell House, or Lissadell Court as it was originally called, was completed in 1837, built largely with stones taken from the Ardtermon and Ballinfull (Doonfore) old castles, and faced with Ballisodare limestone. The architect was Francis Goodwin, and it is in a Grecian Revival style, plain apart from the attractive curved bow in the centre of the south wall, and a Porte-Cochere at the north-facing front door. It is open to the public and well worth a visit. It has a large gallery with excellent acoustics lit by a clerestory and skylights, and an attractive bow drawingroom facing the sea, which has been immortalised by Yeats in his

Lissadell House soon after it was built - By kind permission of Sir Josslyn Gore-Booth

poem which begins:

"Light of evening Lissadell
Great windows open to the South,"(14).

There is a subway leading to the basement, a feature of some large Irish houses, to allow the servants to come and go unobtrusively. The house contains memorabilia of Constance Markievicz, Eva Gore-Booth, and their father Sir Henry's Arctic expeditions. See the illustration above of the house when recently built, and also the design for a very fancy gatelodge which was never built.

Lissadell Gatelodge designed by F. Goodwin which was never built
Courtesy of Local History Collection, County Sligo Library

THE PARKE AND JONES FAMILIES AND OTHERS

The Parke family of Dunally had been enriched with the lands of Murtagh Bacagh O'Connor of Dunally, and there was an old castle there. Roger Parke claimed the lands in lieu of soldier's pay at the end of the seventeenth century. A William Parke of Dunally was High Sherriff of Sligo in 1686. They were a Kent family originally.

Dunally House today

Parke's elder son, Captain Roger Parke, built Newtown, what is now known as Parke's Castle, turning the old O'Rourke castle there into a fortified Stuart house. This is at the edge of Lough Gill in Co. Leitrim and beautifully renovated by the Office of Public Works, open to the public and well worth a visit. The cadet branch stayed in Dunally, and were there until the twentieth century, while the Newtown branch of Parkes died out, their elder daughter Anne, marrying Sir Francis Gore, who inherited the property.

The Jones family also came to Sligo at this time, but less is known about them. From the one adventurer, who was the first Mayor of Sligo, sprang a number of branches in Sligo, living at Benada, Streedagh, Mt. Edward, Springfield, Johnsport, Cargin and Doonfore. Thomas Jones who built Streedagh House in 1724-5 was the grandson of Sir Roger Jones the first arrival.

The Sodens of Grange were a third family arriving at this time, gaining their land, according to an old story, by happening to meet a prospective landowner who had come to see his newly purchased land in North Sligo, and showing him his acres with a sweep of his arm at Munninane; the new landowner decided it looked too boggy and sold it for sixpence to Soden, who proceeded to try to evict O'Hart from the castle. When O'Hart refused to leave, Soden is supposed to have ended the stalemate by hanging O'Hart.

In 1611 the new bishop, Edward King, repaired Elphin cathedral at his own expense. Although a native of Huntingdonshire, he was educated at Trinity College Dublin, obtaining a D.D., and he also built a castle at Elphin to serve him and his successors as an episcopal residence, and recovered many of the ancient lands. He was noted for the sanctity of his life(15), and described as " a truly royal bishop" in a letter from Strafford, then Lord Lieutenant, to Archbishop Laud of Canterbury. He visited Drumcliffe and found the church,"formerly a fair Church", in a bad state of repair, and suggested uniting the parishes of Calry, Drumcliffe and Ahamlish so that the cost of repair could be shared.(16) The suggestion was not taken up.

The next Vicar after Hugo Hohy, William Roycroft, was appointed in 1622 and stayed at Drumcliffe for 42 years, and lived through the tragedy of the 1641 rebellion. See four sections ahead. He was said to be a good divine and preacher.(17)

WHO OWNED THE LAND IN THE SEVENTEENTH CENTURY?

We are fortunate to have a record of the rentals of Sligo properties in the years 1633-1636.(18) Quite a number of mills are mentioned in the area, including Ballincar, which was still standing in the nineteenth century. Seven of the mills were owned by Sir Roger Jones. Eight townlands were owned by the O'Connor family and some land by the O'Harts and one townland by a Mr. Crowe of Dublin. All these properties were set to undertenants.

Ballynagalliagh was an interesting case. It was owned by Lord Clanricard, who set it to a Galway merchant, who in turn set it to Brian O'Connor, who in turn set it to undertenants, for the usual rent plus twelve days' work and a *cosher* at Christmas. *Coshers* were parties that landlords expected tenants to give for the landlord at the tenant's expense. Not a popular idea, but also not a new one, and not a Protestant one either, it had been the tradition for hundreds of years. There was also a good leadmine near the sea at Rosses, owned by the Bishop of Elphin. Andrew O'Crean owned land at Ahamlish, and many of the landed proprietors had mortgaged their lands to him. Captain Charles Colles was the landlord of Cloonderry, Rahaberna and Tully.

LADY O'CONNOR

In the 1630's large tracts of Drumcliffe and Ahamlish - except for a few townlands in Ahamlish owned and sublet by John Ridge Esq., a son in law of Sir Roger Jones - comprising the townlands of Cashelgarron, Munninane, Urlar, Barnaribbon and Lissadell, were owned by Lady O'Connor and her daughter Lady Cressey, as a jointure from the former's late husband Sir Donough O'Connor. This first lady was Eleaner née Butler , the widow of the last Earl of Desmond, and still called "the Countess" locally.

She had led a most interesting life, recorded in her biography written by Anne Chambers.(19) She travelled to London several times to petition the Queen, and her husband was the rebel Earl, imprisoned in the tower. Her tomb can be seen in Sligo Abbey. To give an idea of what the land was like then, Lissadell then was set by her and the rent included goodly portions of butter, wheat, 10 sheep a year, 50 horses a year and 30 horse boys. It was recorded to be good arable land with good turf, and 50 workmen; 10 days worth of mowing. It would graze 200 cows.

In 1615 some people maintained that Lady O'Connor actually had no right to all these acres of O'Connor Sligo territory. Sir Faithful Fortescue, the guardian of the ten-year-old Charles O'Connor, the new Lord of Sligo, brought a law-suit against her. Accounts of the outcome vary, but according to Anne Chambers she fought it tooth and nail, and the court found in her favour. Her detractors then sat back and decided to wait for for her to die instead. But she lived to such a ripe old age that she outlived them all!(20)

STATE OF THE COUNTRYSIDE

The physical state of the countryside was worse in the seventeenth century than now. Much of the woodland still remained, especially in Benbulben and Glencar. Wood-Martin quotes a Scottish traveller, Lithgow, who was travelling in Ireland in 1619-1620, as saying that there were "more rivers, lakes, brooks, strands, quagmires, bogs and marshes in Ireland than in all Christendom besides", and complained that he had to swim his horse across streams and often sunk up to the girths in boggy roads!

Wolves were still around then, and there was a peregrine falcon nesting on Benbulben. The gentry lived in thatched houses then, unless they had a castle; and Drumcliffe Church certainly had a thatched roof at this period, until well into the eighteenth century.

REBELLION AGAIN; COMMONWEALTH DAYS

1n 1641 there started a major and bloody rebellion, during which Sligo suffered very badly. Some basic causes were dissatisfaction that more and more of the territory was going to the planters, that the Plantation Commissioners were acting unfairly, and that the Church of Ireland bishops were attempting to claim lands which had formerly belonged to the Church.

There were atrocities on both sides - a massacre of 38 Protestants who had been admitted to the gaol for safety; followed by a retaliation in the form of the wholesale burning of the town by Sir Frederick Hamilton. Then there was more shameful behaviour the following year from several members of the Coote family, Sir Charles Coote President of Connaught (who was killed at Trim after warming his hands at a fire his son made him by burning the miraculous statue of the Virgin Mary), his brother Richard, (later Lord Coloony), and his son also Sir Charles Coote (later Earl of Mountrath). This last Coote accepted the surrender of the Sligo soldiers but then stripped and killed all of them. The loyalty of the town alternated between Parliamentarians and Royalists for ten long years, but on the whole was loyal to the English King Charles I. They then paid dearly for that loyalty when Cromwell arrived in the country in 1649, though he only stayed nine months. The population was completely decimated, those who had not been killed by soldiers succumbing to famine and plague. About 500,000 people died, out of a population of only two million.

Roman Catholics had their property confiscated, unless they could prove that they had supported Parliament. They were then sent to Connaught to estates of supposedly equal value, except for a four mile wide surrounding stretch reserved for Parliamentarian soldiers who were supposed to keep them confined. This stretch of land went round the whole of Connaught, and was known as 'The Mile Line'. It was gradually reduced in area, first to three miles and then to one mile. Protestants unable to prove their innocence were merely fined. Then Cromwellian officers and adventurers were allowed to buy the confiscated lands, initially for only between four and twelve shillings an acre, but later the price increased substantially. The Cromwellians built a new castle in Sligo in 1653 on the site of the present Town Hall; this was known as the Stone Fort.

It was a troubled and tragic time. For 19 years the Church of Ireland was in disarray, from 1641 until 1660. Cromwell, a Dissenter, filled the church and state offices with his own supporters, mostly Baptists, and deprived the Church of Ireland of any financial support from tithes. He brought in his Free Church ministers. The Cromwellians wanted to abolish episcopacy and the use of the Book of Common Prayer.

They paid 376 "ministers of the gospel", among whom were only 65 Church of Ireland ministers, the ones who had agreed to the state-imposed conditions - they must not wear surplices, use the Book of Common Prayer or use the sign of the cross in Baptism. A committee was set up for the 'Approbation and Trial of Ministers'. The Church of Ireland continued in secret, and we do not know if Drumcliffe was able to continue. William Roycroft had been vicar in 1619; and the next recorded vicar after him was Robert Browne after the Restoration, in 1661,(21) but the records do not show if there was a gap.

Many of Cromwell's Ironsides disbanded in Sligo in 1653, and descended from those veterans would be old Drumcliffe yeoman families like the Irwins, Barbers, Hunters, Littles, Hughes, Halls, Armstrongs, McKims, and Gillmores.

THE RESTORATION

In 1660 came the Restoration of the English Monarchy with the return of King Charles II from exile. The Cromwellian atrocities were now over. Amongst the people to whom land was regranted were local landowners Charles Colles of Rahaberna, Tully and Cloonderry, the Sodens and the Erasmus Smith Trustees who owned land in Lislahelly, Glencarbury and Loughanelteen. A new bishop came to Elphin, one John Parker who had had a rather dramatic life up to then, having been thrown into prison by the Cromwellians on suspicion of being a spy for the Marquis of Ormond, who was working for the Royalist cause. The

Marquis secured Parker's release in exchange for another prisoner. Parker was his chaplain.

Parker later became Archbishop of Tuam and then of Dublin. He repaired the cathedral and the palace. He appointed Robert Browne as successor to Roycroft in 1661. Browne came to Drumcliffe from having been Vicar of Taunagh (Riverstown), only twenty miles away. He and Rycroft were both Prebendaries of Drumcliffe. Browne was the last to hold that title as the prebend appears to have lapsed. He seems to have been a pluralist, as during some of the time he was Vicar of Drumcliffe he was also Archdeacon of Killala and Prebendary of Raphoe. But one must not be too quick to condemn this practice, as money was so short that often it was the only way to have enough to live on and support a family.

One of the events in the parish in Browne's day was that the twice-year-ly Carney fair was started for selling cows, sheep, pigs and horses, on a three acre site in the townland of Cullaghmore. Carney earned a reputation in those days for bloody faction fights. Carney fair would start very early, at 6 am., and by the evening, sales concluded in the traditional Irish manner, the skirmishing would begin. Carney was said to be an important place in those times; and on into the nineteenth century it was still, having a tailor, a blacksmith, a baker and a private school. There were 45 houses actually in the village in 1837. Seven years later than Carney's fair, also in the seventeenth century, Grange too had a fair, presided over by the Soden family. It was not until the nineteenth century that Cliffoney had a fair.

Drumcliffe seems to have been fairly prosperous in those days, for the religious census of the Diocese of Elphin conducted in 1659 records that there were working mills in the area and a wealth of tradesmen - shoemakers, carpenters, millers, bleachers, smiths, gardeners, tailors, cowherds, weavers and coopers - but, as today, mostly farmers.(22)

JACOBITES AND WILLIAMITES

James Read came as Vicar of Drumcliffe and Ahamlish in 1674.(23) He stayed for forty-nine years, which would have given a good measure of stability to the parish. His Bishop was Bishop Simon Digby of Elphin, who was a miniaturist, and also connected with the Digby family of Sherborne. A portrait and a miniature of Bishop Digby are to be seen in Sherborne Castle today.

Read would have seen much bloodshed during the Jacobite-Williamite wars, between the supporters of King James II of England and William of Orange his son-in-law. Among the officers appointed to fight on the Williamite side from the parish were several names which could have been parishioners, or their relatives elsewhere in the county if not: Lt. Matthew Ormsby, Capt. Jeremiah Jones, Cornet Duke Ormsby, Capt. William Ormsby and Ensign William Parkes. One officer, Dr. John Lesley, sent his wife and children to Inishmurray for safety.

There were several sieges. In 1688 there was the Siege of Sligo when Patrick Sarsfield captured the Cromwellian castle from St. Sauvent, a Williamite officer. This siege lasted four days, and the siege machine known as a 'sow' was used.

Grange was garrisoned at this time, by the Jacobites, the old O'Hart castle providing a strategic point. Tiffan, the Williamite officer in charge at Ballyshannon, just across the order into Co. Donegal, attacked the castle, and just as success was in sight an explosion occurred, with the loss of much life. The explosion is thought by some to have been set off by the defenders themselves, but the Revd William Henry writing in 1739 has given us the full story. A small party of English were passing that way, and made a show of attacking the castle. One of them, going under the wall of the castle, threw a grenade in at a small window. It fell into the powder-room which in a moment blew up the castle from the foundation and all the garrison perished, except for one man who was dragged half-dead out of the ruins.(24)

Francis Gore, the second son of Sir Francis Gore of Ardtermon, was in charge of a troop of men fighting on the Williamite side, and he managed to save many civilian lives by sending his prisoners ahead of him to warn their friends in Sligo of the approach of the Derry and Enniskillen troops, and so the town was able to be evacuated first and taken without bloodshed.

Lord Mitchelburne who had been one of the Williamite defenders of Derry marched to Sligo to besiege the Sod Fort, later renamed the Green Fort. This was a fort built in a prominent position on the hill to the north on the site of an old fort called Rath na Bhriotog, or fort of the British women, according to the Annals of the Four Masters. The fort was defended manfully by the governor of Sligo, hunchbacked 70 year-old Sir Teigue O'Regan; it is often called Sir Teigue O'Regan's fort to this day. Mitchelburne and his men encamped one night in Drumcliffe parish, and then set up their camp in an old fort that the men set to repairing. It was on a hill more or less opposite the Greenfort, usually described as being Rathbraughan Fort, although the modern Ordnance Survey map marks the smaller Lisnalurg fort as the Williamite camp. Excavations for a new stretch of main road (the new Bundoran road) revealed many bones from this period. Reinforcements to the Williamite side arrived over the Curlews under Lord Granard, and Mitchelburne had by then captured the outworks of the Green Fort and O'Regan, having held the fort for fifteen months, and come off badly in a skirmish in Ballisodare, surrendered honourably, just before the Treaty of Limerick.

Although it is true that a great many Roman Catholics supported King James in the hope of regaining their confiscated lands, there was not a one-to-one correspondence between peoples' religious allegiance and their political allegiance in this war. Many Protestant gentry also fought for King James, and William of Orange employed many Roman Catholic mercenary soldiers.

DRUMCLIFFE - The Church of Ireland Parish in its North Sligo Setting.

52

PART V: THE EIGHTEENTH CENTURY.

SOME MORE PARISH FAMILIES

Among other county families living in the parish during the eighteenth century were the Jones's of Streedagh, Carney, Mt Edward, Springfield, Raughley and Johnsfort or Johnsport near Lissadell (all sprung from Thomas Jones the grandson of Sir Roger Jones the first arrival who built St. John's Sligo); the Temples, who owned much of Mullaghmore; the Gethins of Court; the Irwins of Willowbrook; the Ormsbys of Belvoir; the Hillasses of Cregg House & Philip Byrne of Cregg. As well as the Parkes, Gores and Sodens already mentioned, there were Todds, Nicholsons and O'Sullevans, Charles Colles, Manus Leneghan and Thomas Osborne.

Many of these played their part in community affairs, taking turns being High Sheriff for the county, a position entailing much responsibility and expense. Their duties included selecting and appointing a Grand Jury, building jails and roads, collecting taxes, local government duties and entertaining Judges. Other High Sheriffs mentioned in the eighteenth century were Captain Humphrey Griffith of Ballincar Castle, a relation of the Irwins of Tanrego. The Griffiths became a numerous family and spread to Ballytivnan as well; Captain Griffith's brother was the Very Revd. Richard Griffiths, Dean of Ross; and another brother, Edward, married Elizabeth Lawrence, daughter of Queen Anne's state physician. Some members of these Parish families, including Sir John Temple and Sir Francis Gore, served as members of Parliament.

The Ormsbys were an English family from Lincolnshire who came over in the reign of Elizabeth the First. The Gethins of Ballindoon in South Sligo and also of Court were Members of Parliament for the Borough, but inclined to be absentee landlords. They owned Rathcormack House, but leased it to the O'Byrnes. The Gethins, Gores, Sodens, Ormsbys and Wynnes (of whom more later) were all interrelated by marriage.

SOME NOTABLE CHARACTERS

Thomas Soden of Grange was notable for his longevity. He lived in three centuries, being born in 1592, and dying in 1713 at the age of 121. He was High Sheriff of Co. Sligo when he was 82. His great great grandson Thomas Soden J.P. of Moneygold was Provost of Sligo (Mayor) for 33 years, from 1785 to 1818. His diary has survived, and gives an insight into the commercial prosperity of Sligo at that time. John McTernan has a complete chapter on him in his book "In Sligo Long Ago", he was quite a character by all accounts. James Soden too lived to a good, age, dying in his 109th year.

The Parkes became very numerous, and had a castle in Glencar as well as Dunally and Newtown on Lough Gill. One branch boasted the famous late nineteenth century Surgeon Major Thomas Heazle Parke who was the first

Irishman to cross Africa, going with Stanley's expedition as its doctor. He was a specialist in tropical diseases, and was from the the the branch of the Parke family in the neighbouring county of Cavan, living in Kilmore.

LIFE IN THE EIGHTEENTH CENTURY

The eighteenth century was one of comparative peace and prosperity as far as wars and fighting were concerned. It was the golden age of Irish Georgian building when Ireland still had her own parliament, and gifted speakers in it like Burke and Grattan, who were able to present Ireland's case eloquently. It was also a century of danger, difficulty and crime. Murders were common, as were duels, cock-fighting and piracy; shipwrecks were common at sea and travelling by road was rendered dangerous by highwaymen, and the job of the hearthmoney tax-collectors was fraught with danger.

Saltworks were established in the parish in the second half of the eighteenth century, and salt pans are marked on old maps on the river estuary in Coolbeg townland. Landlords were at this time busy trying to establish a linen industry, and several bleach greens are marked on old maps, after 1750, at Ballincar and Kilsellagh. By 1798 there were twelve bleach yards in Sligo town.(1) The shapes of the lazy beds can still be detected beyond Lisnalurg on the hilly field below the small fort. There were flax mills at Ballincar, Millbrook and Grange. There was a corn mill at Ballincar as well, with a little quay for exporting the grain by ship. These mills were owned by the Wynne family; they are gone now, but see the sketch of the Ballincar Mills done by a member of the family in 1838.

The linen industry was very labour intensive, and employed men, women and children for the many laborious jobs necessary, from ploughing, harrowing, clodding, weeding, pulling and binding; to watering, carrying, spreading, lifting, drying, beetling, scutching, heckling, spinning, quilling, warping and winding. It was mostly brown linen, which could then be sold to bleachers who treated it and sold it on to Dublin merchants or foreign buyers.

The Simpson family owned the flax mill at Millbrook, which was a watermill, as was the flax mill at Grange. The present owner of the Millbrook property, Brenda Anderson, recounts that the well-built wall along the garden and courtyard cost the original owners one penny an hour to have constructed. Patrick Meldrum grew flax at the base of Benbulben, at Keelty, and had half an acre planted, for which he qualified for an award of two spinningwheels, under the Premium scheme, as did Philip McKim. The Shaws, Lindsays, Barbers, Hendersons, Cunninghams and Henrys only qualified for one spinningwheel, having only a quarter of an acre planted with flax. The industry never had the same success as that in the north of Ireland, and this has been attributed to the water, which is very hard in this limestone district, and so less suitable for the process; the strong smell may have had a hand in it too! Irish flax is also considered rather coarse, and the finer Belgian flax is imported for the linen industry in

Pencil sketch of the Mills at Ballincar - 1838 Drawing by John Arthur Wynne

Northern Ireland today.

The government were offering bounties to encourage fisheries in the second half of this century and many landlords were starting to take more interest in their estates and to build workers' cottages. The oyster beds in the bay were well known, and the Revd. W. Henry writing in 1739 declared that the oysters from the oysterbeds at Sligo and Drumcliffe were to be "reckoned for firmness, fatness and delicious taste to excel all others".(2) Embroidery, ropes, candles and snuff are also listed among the industries of this century.

Taxes were severe in this century. There was even a tax on hearths on the principle that if people owned one or more hearths they were wealthy enough to be taxed. Other taxes payable to the State were the Window Tax and the Jury Tax, also the Cess Tax which was administered by the Church of Ireland; two members of the vestry would be appointed as applotters, who applotted the cess due from each farmer towards the upkeep of the roads and the Militia. Tithes on the other hand were payable in kind, and only those on large crops were collected, except that traditionally certain families would supply eggs or potatoes or milk to the rectory.

EIGHTEENTH CENTURY CLERGY OF THE PARISH AND DIOCESE

Eubule Ormsby became vicar of both Drumcliffe and Ahamplish (a common spelling of it then) in 1723, residing in Drumcliffe.(3) He came from a local landed family. After seven years of ministry there he went on to be Vicar of St. John's Sligo. He was succeeded by Edward Munns, who was Vicar of

Drumcliffe only, and who was also Archdeacon. Munns was also from a local landed family, and was a cousin of Oliver Goldsmith's. He died in office after 26 years.(4)

Munns's bishop for part of his incumbency was Bishop Edward Synge. This large man, over six feet tall, was a generous philanthropist, an improving farmer and a man of wide interests. His letters to his daughter Alicia, the only one of his seven children to survive, give us a valuable glimpse of life at the Palace at Elphin during this period.(5)

Like Parker and Hodson before him, he found a ruinous cathedral, and rebuilt it with the help of First Fruits money. This was a fund which was based on the old 'Annates' tax - the first fruits of a clergyman's labours - which had in the days before the Reformation gone to the Pope, and went to the English Crown after the Reformation. We owe it to Dean Jonathan Swift of St. Patrick's Cathedral Dublin, the well-known writer and satirist, that he negotiated to get this fund transferred to the Church of Ireland, as without it the majority of country churches could not have been built.

Synge was no absentee but actually did visitations round the parishes, some of which he was obliged to cancel because of bad weather. He grew flax and kept four horses and a mule, and according to his letters his life was very taken up with such things as manuring, scytheing, raking, buying cattle, servant problems (he employed seventeen) tailors, wine-merchants, pet dogs and ornamental fowl. A sermon he preached at St. Andrew's Church Dublin before the House of Commons, received a vote of thanks in the house. The subject of the sermon was "Toleration".

The Bishop's Palace at Elphin - By kind permission of the Irish Architectural Archive

PENAL TIMES

The eighteenth century was also notorious for the Penal Laws, which were extremely rigorous in their naked theory, but thankfully not enforced in every area of Ireland. These laws were first enacted in 1695, and one is glad to know that a lot of the Church of Ireland bishops protested strongly against them.

Roman Catholics were denied the vote, and not permitted to enter university or parliament or the professions, or be schoolteachers, or to own a horse worth more than five pounds, and any Protestant was allowed to accost a Catholic and buy their horse for five pounds, and the Militia could seize their horses and wagons. Sending children to be educated abroad was not permitted - but many did it. They were to be fined £60 a month if they did not attend the Church of Ireland services. They were not permitted to own firearms, or to travel more than five miles away from their homes. Property had to be subdivided between all the sons rather than passed down to just one son - this one was a real poverty trap, and led to smaller and smaller holdings. And if a priest was discovered in the country he was to be hanged.

Masses were not allowed to be heard in churches and the mass rocks come from this era. There used to be an old mass house at Bun Breunoige near Lissadell, between 1746 and 1756, and there is also a mass rock at Gorteen near Ballintrillick. The Mass Rock at Streedagh is particularly interesting. It was the roof of one of the chambers of the court tomb there, very much an altar shape. From that hill the neighbouring hills of Lang's Hill, Hud's Hill and Burns Hill can be seen well, and signals used to pass in this way, using a blazing sod of oil-soaked turf, from Sligo to Rosses Point to Raughley to Knocklane to Mt. Edward to Streedagh to Moneygold to Mullaghmore, to warn the priests if the Militia were after them, so that they could disband the flock and hide.(6)

'On Garland Sunday, the last Sunday in July, the tradition of mass rocks is commemorated, and the ancient holy place of Tobernault near Lough Gill is one place amongst others where Sligo people still have an open air mass once yearly, and rosaries are said there for peace regularly now, as a recent development. 'Hedge Schools' come from this time too, sometimes held in hedges but more often in barns and sheds or farmhouse kitchens. The Hedge School masters were often very well educated on the Continent, and taught Latin and classical literature as well as more basic subjects.

The penal laws can often give a false impression however of the life of the Church of Ireland and it must in honesty be pointed out that laws against the Roman Catholics holding their own masses did not mean that they frequented the Church of Ireland, they only did this when necessary, to have their marriages legalised. Again, although tithes were supposed to be paid to the Church of Ireland clergyman, often they were not, and these men did suffer a degree of hardship, and their own churches were by no means as full as we would imagine, or in as good state of repair. Rectors were still holding several livings together and leaving their curates to do the work, and many of them were not even living in their parishes.

An example of this is the Revd Eugene O'Connor, who in Elizabethan times had three other livings besides Drumcliffe, stretching to Achonry and Skreen; a clergyman with a motorcar would find such a wide area very difficult today, so on horseback it must have been impossible to offer to people any standard of pastoral care. Minevoriske, as the name of his Drumcliffe Rectory was called then, was described as being 'between the two bridges'.(7)

THE GREAT FROST

Edward Munns saw great hardship during his incumbency, for he lived during the time of The Great Frost which covered much of Europe in 1740, leading to a famine dubbed by the historian of the Great Frost, David Dickson, as "the forgotten famine".(8) The dramatic weather lasted from December 1739 through to September 1741, and the great frost was the longest period of extreme cold known to modern European history. It was as low as 10 degrees Fahrenheit, liquids froze indoors and there were ice-floes in the river mouths, even the street lights were snuffed out by the intense cold. Rivers and lakes froze.

After the initial novelty of carnivals and banquets on the ice had worn off, people realised the reality of it all - animals died in the fields, the water mills could not operate, coal soared in price and, worst of all for the poor, the potatoes went to mush. When the frost disappeared in February, the cold stayed, with piercing northerly winds and no Spring rains. There was then a drought in the Spring and Summer of 1741 followed by a very bad harvest. Tempestuous weather started again in September, with snow until December and then downpours and flooding. Sligo appears to have been one of the worst-hit places, as there were food riots here in the summer of 1740 and in April 1741.(9)

Much philanthropic work was no doubt carried on unrecorded; the Church of Ireland parishes would have been at the spearhead of relief efforts. They acted as a sort of lowest hierarchical level of local government. Many obelisks and roads and monuments were built at this time to provide work and food, but many were too weak to work, and suffering from smallpox, dysentery, typhus and fever. This is probably the origin of the two pairs of unusual stone pillars in Lisnalurg townland, erected it is thought under the supervision of the Scottish steward of the Wynne Estate, who lived at Auburn House (now Lisnalurg House). The lower road connecting the main Bundoran road to Ballincar could well have been named "Scotsman's Walk" after this gentleman.

The Sligo food rioters were successful in preventing a shipload of barley going to Limerick. It is disappointing that the parish records for this period have been destroyed in the Four Courts fire in Dublin during the Civil War in 1922. But it is estimated that about one cottager in three died at this time, and many of the mass graves that can be seen outside churches date from this time rather than the nineteenth century famine.

PARSONS DOHERTY, CURTIS, OBINS AND COWPER

In 1756 Richard Doherty, a Cork man, became vicar.(10) He was the son of Colonel Letham Doherty, and was educated at Trinity College Dublin, entering at the age of fifteen. Discussions at Vestry meetings during his incumbency were mostly concerned with overseeing the upkeep of the roads, church vestries then being very much part, as we saw, of local government. Philip Birne and John Keough oversaw a road which included the fearsat across the strand. Doherty died after only five years in Drumcliffe.

In 1760 the new incumbent Robert Curtis arrived, and he was Vicar of both Drumcliffe and Taunagh (Riverstown) at the same time.(11) From the Vestry records it appears that he favoured Taunagh with his presence more often, and left his curate Andrew Knox in charge of Drumcliffe. He only chaired six meetings in that time. Under their joint leadership the churchwardens were asked to repair the windows and re-thatch the roof. However it was eventually decided, in 1762, to rebuild the church instead, with a timber and slate roof. To save money on the new church, which the builders never completed fully, they hit on a rather clever idea. Instead of buying pews, they marked out sections on the church floor, a section per family; each family was then expected to build their own pew or else forfeit their patch! Andrew Knox was curate under both Doherty and Curtis, but by the time Mr. Obins arrived he had gone to be in charge of Ahamlish. He was at Ahamlish during the 1766 religious census, when only eight Protestants were recorded in that parish, and 107 Roman Catholics.

Michael Obins was the next Vicar, in 1767.(12) He was the son of Anthony Obins of Portadown. He was a scholar in Trinity College Dublin, and came to Drumcliffe at the age of 58, having held several other posts previously, Castlemacadam and Thurles amongst them. He died in Drumcliffe and there are two graveslabs or tablets to him and to his son the Revd Anthony Obins on the outer wall of the vestry at the back of the church, which would suggest that they are buried in the graveyard, and that the slabs were mounted there when the new church was built. Sir Booth Gore and Philip Birne were churchwardens five years in succession, Sir Booth remaining as Rector's Warden, and Philip Birne (or Burns) as Peoples' Warden. The bishop for the first half of his incumbency was Jemmet Browne, who came from having been Bishop of Cork, where he was a very good friend of the well-known philosopher Bishop George Berkeley of Cloyne. Browne later became Archbishop of Tuam.

During Obins's time, the road from Lisnalurg to Carney needed repairing, and this was achieved by six days' labour from the whole parish. Also during his incumbency, in 1780, Rosses Point was raided by pirates who made off with *The Swallow*, a local fishing boat, after loading her with pillage. The previous year there had been some excitement over some French privateers sighted off Inishmurray, but they turned out to be landing sick men and taking fresh water on board. The Rector's son, Anthony Obins, was curate for a while, and the Revd Hugh Johnston took over from him in 1782. During the Obins's time, the current fear was always of invasion by the French. So in 1778 the Irish National Volunteer Force was created, with the object of being ready to repel invasion. Most of the officers were Protestants, but many Roman Catholics supported it, and some were secretly admitted as members. Charles Dodgson, the grandfather of the author of "Alice in Wonderland", became bishop for the last eight years of Michael Obins's incumbency.

Thomas Cowper, Obins's successor, resigned after only two years and went to minister at Taunagh instead! He arrived in 1783 and departed in 1785(13). His curate was Hugh Johnston, and the two men appear to have encouraged the work of supporting foundlings and widows. Foundlings were abandoned children, who had by law to be looked after by the Church of Ireland, and who also were obliged to become Church of Ireland members. During these next two decades, the 1780's and the 1790's, a great many of the Penal Laws were repealed, but the laws prohibiting Roman Catholics from voting or from sitting in Parliament were still in force.

PARSONS RADCLIFFE AND WYNNE

The next vicar was slightly more permanent, staying in the parish for twelve years. He was the Reverend Stephen Radcliffe, later Canon Radcliffe, who came in 1785.(14) During his incumbency numbers would seem to have been increasing, as the Vestry decided in 1790 that an "immediate enlargement of the church was necessary"(15), adding cautiously that the enlargement should not cost more than £40 a year. William Barber, William Parke and Johnston Shaw were Radcliffe's 'right hand men'. During Radcliffe's time the tithe applotters record that the common or fair green of Carney was to be exempt from the cess tax. It is interesting to note that this fair field still has a good wall around it, and Jim Barber of Carney recollects that when he was young people used to come from about four neighbouring counties for the fair, which would last almost a week, and they would camp in the fair field in readiness the night before.

During Canon Radcliffe's incumbency the Drumcliffe Infantry was formed, in 1796. Their captain was Arthur Irwin of Willowbrook, who had just completed his year as High Sheriff of Co. Sligo. The 1st. and 2nd. Lieutenants were William O'Beirne and Samuel Shaw who were also churchwardens at Drumcliffe Church. The formation of the new regiment was necessitated by the menace posed by a secret society known as the Defenders, who intimidated people and stole arms from their houses. In 1794 they had been particularly active and the government had suggested the formation of local yeomanry regiments to supplement the already existing Militia. At this time there was a mail-coach making the journey between Sligo and Dublin; it was copper-lined, not just for warmth, but against bullets! (16)

A new vicar was appointed in 1797, the year before the 1798 rising. He was The Reverend Richard Wynne(17), who came from the Wynne family of Haslewood, which is today in the parish of Calry. Successive heads of the Wynne family played quite a part in Drumcliffe parish affairs, as they had extensive property in the parish. The Wynne family were of Welsh origin and the first Wynne, Owen, to arrive in Ireland came in 1658 during the Protectorship of Richard Cromwell to take up the offer of two leases of church lands in Co. Leitrim which he later bought. He was an older son, and inherited a property in Wales as well. He later became a colonel in the army under Charles II. One of his sons, Owen, purchased an estate in Sligo for £20,000, in 1722, and built Haslewood in 1731, a Palladian mansion consisting of a central three-storey block with curved sweeps or quadrants leading to two two-storey wings, and a venetian window above the front door. It is near the shore of Lough Gill, and said to be the earliest surviving Irish house designed by Richard Cassells, the architect also of Leinster House, Powerscourt and St. John's Church, Sligo, and others.

Richard ministered in the parish for 14 years, until the arrival of John Yeats as Rector. Yeats had been in Drumcliffe already as curate, around the year 1802. The parish seems to have been well organised under Richard Wynne. They now had a parish clerk for the first time. He was Thomas Gibson, who was also the schoolmaster. He was appointed in 1803. The churchwardens took very seriously the aspect of their job which involved making sure the parishioners attended church. At the Easter Vestry in 1806 it was reported that churchwardens Samuel Shaw and Christopher Meldrum "discharged their duty with diligence and fidelity, especially in enforcing the laws for the due observance of the Sabbath"(18)

THE 1798 RISING

The last major event of the eighteenth century was the 1798 rising, initiated by the United Irishmen, a band of men throughout Ireland including several Church of Ireland and Presbyterian members amongst their leadership, who sought the aid of the French in their fight for freedom. Rebellion was already brewing locally, with nocturnal meetings, and smiths making pikes secretly, and Irwin's haggard was burnt (actually a very moderate act compared to what was happening in other parts of Ireland). The Bishop, Dr. John Law, was obliged to to raise a troop of soldiers for the defence of his district; it was commanded by the archdeacon.

A small French force landed at Killala under General Humbert, and were joined by United Irishmen volunteers. The French and the Irish were finally defeated at Vinegar Hill in Wexford, after a skirmish in Sligo at Carrignagat near Collooney. There were heroes on both sides at Collooney. Major Ormsby and Colonel Vereker commanded the English forces, and Vereker it was who made his men wear the yellow ragwort or *buchulain* flowers in their buttonholes to distinguish them from their opponents. Captain Bartholomew Teeling was one of the heroes of the Irish side. Teeling was a leading member of the United Irishmen from Lisburn in Ulster, who served as a captain in General Humbert's army. Following the defeat of the rising, in spite of General Humbert's efforts to obtain

DRUMCLIFFE - The Church of Ireland Parish in its North Sligo Setting.

—————— 61 ——————

for him the same honourable treatment as the French-born officers, he was sentenced to death and executed at Arbour Hill in Dublin.

There is a monument commemorating Teeling outside the village of Collooney and the Erin statue in Market street Sligo also commemorates 1798. There are cannon balls and other memorabilia of the 1798 rising in the Sligo Museum in Stephen Street.

DRUMCLIFFE - The Church of Ireland Parish in its North Sligo Setting.

62

PART VI: THE EARLY NINETEENTH CENTURY

AFTERMATH OF THE REBELLION

Things quietened down after the 1798 rebellion more quickly in Drumcliffe, as it did not suffer from the reprisals that were felt in west Sligo. Only two families were awarded compensation for damages caused that year, Patrick Coulter of Ballinfull to the tune of £10.16.11/2, and Francis Beolan of Tully, to the tune of £6.10s.(1). Andrew Parke of the The Carberry Cavalry and Lt. Samuel Shaw of the Drumcliffe and Caulrey Cavalry, and no doubt other parishioners too, would have returned to the parish as heroes.

The rector's brother, the Rt. Hon. Owen Wynne, had been in action as a Captain of the County Sligo Light Infantry, who had distinguished themselves at Vinegar Hill and then took part in leading the attack on the remaining rebels at Killala. The Yeomanry, who were almost all Protestants, had proved so useful during the rebellion that the government decided to keep them as a permanent force, able to be called on at short notice. Another parishioner, Thomas Soden of Grange, became Captain of the Drumcliffe Infantry, and the Mr. Irwin who had had his haggard burned was Captain of the Drumcliffe Yeomanry.

Change was in the air. The Act of Union had come into effect in January 1801, uniting Ireland with England, and depriving Ireland of her own Parliament. Owen Wynne, together with his fellow M.P.'s for the town and county of Sligo, Edward Cooper and Charles O'Hara, had voted against the Act of Union, which nevertheless was carried by only a small majority of 67 votes, its success due to the expedient of sinecures and titles broadcast widely. But the Catholic Emancipation which it was anticipated would follow the act took another 30 years to come.

LIFE IN THE NINETEENTH CENTURY

Corn at this time was fetching a very high price, and much of the land was put to tillage, rather than sheep. There were corn mills at Drumcliffe, Lislary, Bunduff, Cullaghbeg, Ballintrillick, Collinsford, Willowbrook, Kilsellagh, Grange, Rathbraughan and Ballincar, and the flax mill at Millport was converted to corn. A dam was built to direct the water from the Drumcliffe River to the mill, which was at present day Milltown. The best remains of one of these old water mills is at Rathbraughan. Drumcliffe, Collinsford and Willowbrook also had Tuck mills for treating and finishing cloth.

People lived on potatoes rather than barley and oats which were exported. Woodmartin recounts that every cabin had its dog, but they were none too friendly, and so a law was passed requiring that they should all be attached to a log - but almost impossible to enforce. It was round about this time that the Threshers came into existence, a secret society who blackened their faces and went around punishing Roman Catholics who paid too much to the priest for

DRUMCLIFFE - The Church of Ireland Parish in its North Sligo Setting.

63

services and forcing others not to pay their tithes to the Church of Ireland clergy - thus attacking both denominations. The Penny Boys were a similar movement coming from this, in Mayo and south-west Sligo.

This violence came to a head halfway through the century, and vicars were often evicted at night. But when the Church of Ireland members delivered an ultimatum that if it happened again the parish priest would be treated in the same way, it all stopped abruptly.

The taxes people had to pay were still very high in this century, including tithes to a church they did not belong to, as well as to their own priests. Some people found that the only way they could levy the money was by distilling illicit liquor. The townland of Barnaribbon was one of the main locations of illicit stills - or at least those which were found out!(2) The economy of the island of Inishmurray was particularly dependent on distilling poteen, and a whole garrison of policemen was sent over to deal with the problem there. Later in the century the famous Father Theobald Matthew started up a temperance campaign in Sligo, which calmed things a bit, and may have reduced the previously alarming number of duels that were fought. However these continued on well into the next century. Duellists were brought to court but the trials were said to be mere formalities, and Juries tended to be satisfied if the duel had been conducted according to the rules.(3)

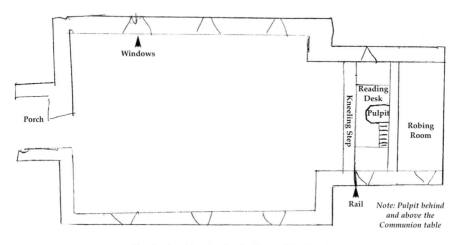

Sketch of architect's plan for Drumcliffe Church

BUILDING A NEW CHURCH

Since 1795, when there had finally been enough money saved to pay an architect, the parishioners had been paying money into the safe keeping of the Revd Richard Wynne for the building of the new church. The churchwardens at the start of the new century were Thomas Barber and Philip McKim. They recorded with pride in 1800 that the sum of £253-10s-1 1/2d had been saved for rebuilding the church.(4) And so the project went ahead, continuing as money became available. The old church we gather was of more modest proportions.

The new church was to seat 300 people. The attendance in 1846 was noted as 120; but this could have been due to the cholera epidemic and successive years of failure of the potato crop having decimated the population.

Drumcliffe Church before and after 1999 renovations

THE STYLE OF THE NEW CHURCH

The plans of the interior show that the style was simple, and rather in the manner of the Methodists, with great centrality being given to the pulpit, which was raised high above and behind the communion table, in front of a windowless east wall. This was to be expected, as the theology of the Church of Ireland at the time was giving prominence to preaching rather than to the administration of the sacrament of Holy Communion. Early in the century the Evangelical Revival was beginning to gather momentum, and having a wide influence. In fact there is other evidence that the influence had reached as far as Drumcliffe. A special mission was held at Drumcliffe church, with the fervent Archdeacon William Digby preaching; and Owen Wynne, the rector's brother, was a generous donor to the new Hibernian Missionary Society when it was founded in 1814.(5) It is interesting to notice that in later alterations at the end of the century the communion table was given more prominence and the pulpit was moved to the side. There were three galleries, with box pews in the side galleries.

However, the crowning glory, the steeple, was still not finally finished in 1805. So four years later in 1809 the vestry were obliged to borrow £738-9s-2 3/4 d. from the Trustees and Commissioners of the Irish First Fruits Board to finish it. The Board of First Fruits was almost a government department, and certainly a force to be reckoned with. They helped many parishes build new churches, but tragically the money was only available to build a new church and not to renovate an old one - much fine church and cathedral architecture has been lost to us in this way.

The typical First Fruits church at its very basic level, was a barn shaped church rendered with lime plaster with no gutters, no heating and sometimes no windows in the North wall. Thankfully Drumcliffe escaped this fate, and had a proper architect, although no record can be found of who designed the 1805 church. There are four handsome limestone piers or pilasters supporting the tower and ending in pinnacles, and an elegant balustrade around the top of the tower, and a generous inward slanting multiple layered pointed arch above the doorway, all of which are marks of Thomas Cooley's style. Cooley had died in 1784, but his book of twelve patterns were a response to his patron Earl-Archbishop Robinson's Act for creating chapels-of-ease. The influence of Cooley's style spread widely throughout Ireland in the following decades,(6) so whoever designed it could well have been influenced by Cooley's styles. Cooley recommended exterior rendering of sand and fresh lime, and ordinary plaster white-washed on the inside walls.(7) There are two string-courses on the tower with rondels between the two on three sides, and louvred belfry windows on all four sides of the tower. The tower windows match the nave windows, all with attractive tracery and hood mouldings. The walls are mainly of sandstone and probably from the older church. There is a relieving arch above the doorway and all the doors and windows are framed in cut and dressed limestone. The trees were planted round the graveyard in 1805.

By 1811, Richard Wynne's final year in the parish, the steeple was completed at last. There is a plaque on the north wall of the tower with his name on it and the date of completion. This was a 'steeple' not in the sense of a spire, but of the high church tower with four pinnacles that we see today. But it was not until 1814 that the really final touches were in place, for a rope for the church bell was purchased that year!

BISHOP LE POER TRENCH

The new bishop, Power le Poer Trench, would no doubt have been a great encourager to finishing the work. He was an energetic man, who took his visitations seriously, riding round his diocese and encouraging building projects, and seeing that the registers were being kept up. This philanthropic and spirited Bishop personally led a detachment of the Enniskillen Dragoons against some rioting Whiteboys, and after his evangelical conversion under the influence of Archdeacon William Digby, he became a promoter of the revival, and a vice-president of the Hibernian Church Missionary Society.(8) He was later to become the last Archbishop of Tuam.

A sad incident happened during his time at Elphin. Owing to his activities as magistrate someone wanted to murder him, and they planned to use a boy who worked in the bishop's household to help them. The boy was to leave one lamp, which was normally extinguished at bed-time, shining as a sign that the bishop had retired. But an old man happened to overhear the murderer's conversation with the boy, and reported it to the bishop, who then personally extinguished the lamp. The tragedy was that the old man who disclosed the plot was himself murdered by the plotter, who then escaped to Canada.(9)

INTER CHURCH RELATIONS

Now that the steeple was completed, money was donated to help the Roman Catholics finish their chapel at Rathcormack, half a mile down the road. The vestry book reports that this was done by a levy of a penny per acre of land. Some gave as generouly as £1, and some 5 shillings. The total cost of the chapel was £500, and the Church of Ireland ruling was that bishops were expected to give £5, rectors £1 and curates ten shillings. A priest bequeathed £100 which must have helped a lot.

But one wonders what the standard of workmanship of the new church at Drumcliffe was, when one reads that only eleven years later the parishioners were obliged to rent the Roman Catholic schoolhouse for their services, as the church was being repaired! It is good to know that relations were already cordial between the churches in this part of the world.

SIZE AND EXTENT OF THE PARISH. MUNNINANE

Drumcliffe was from the start a large parish - large enough to be obliged to raise a cess of 55 guineas to defray the expenses of raising their quota of eleven militiamen.(10) In the mid 1880's O'Rourke notes that the proportion of Protestants to Catholics was unusually high.(11) In 1841 the population of this nine square miles area was 11,946, so judging by the fact that the church seated 300, by 'high' he can only have meant about two-and-a-half per cent of the total population of the area.

At the start of the nineteenth century the parish included lands which were later separated off into independent parishes. This was partly for convenience and partly justified by the numbers. Rosses Point was one, see the story of its founding further on, and Lissadell was another. Rosses Point was later joined to the parish of St. John's, in Sligo town, but Lissadell was to revert to Drumcliffe.

Munninane, however, was always a chapel of ease, built in 1896, motivated by Lissadell Rector Frederick Sheridan Le Fanu because too many parishioners at that end of the parish were attending the new gospel hall that George Siggins had built across the road from his house at Cashelgarron, and so Munninane was built to try and get them back - very successfully it would seem,

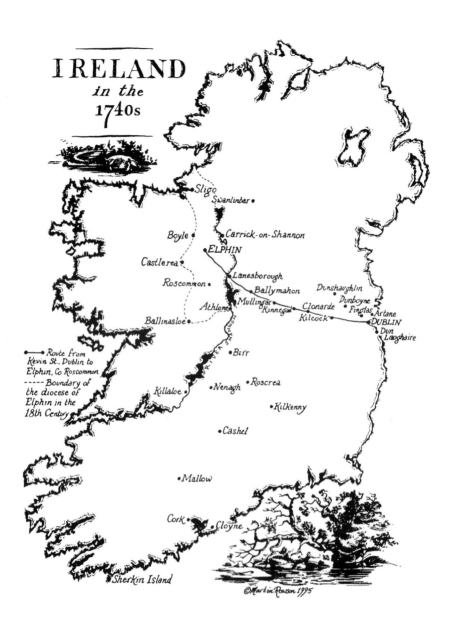

Map of Ireland (re 1740's) showing Elphin Diocese - by kind permission of Martin Rowson

DRUMCLIFFE - The Church of Ireland Parish in its North Sligo Setting.

——— **68** ———

judging by its swelling and loyal population today. It is still part of Lissadell 'grouped parish' within the Drumcliffe group, today. The architect is not known. The little church, known as St. Kevin's, has square-headed single mullioned windows and is rusticated in the style used by J.H.Fuller.

Muninane Church

The gospel hall was built by the members of the Lissadell Methodist church, which used to be well back in the woods behind the school. Cashelgarron Gospel Hall closed in the early 1970's and the building has now become a private dwelling; it is now next door to the Siggins' thatched cottage, owing to the rerouting of the road. The new owners are very proud of it and keep it as much as possible in the correct style with the notice-board and a pulpit. Much earlier, in 1841, Owen Wynne had granted some land for the building of an Erasmus Smith school in the townland, beside the site occupied by the church. This is now a private house. See the section on Munninane School.

AHAMLISH
In 1811 Ahamlish became a separate parish again for a while, with a new church built to accommodate a hundred people, in 1813. Although it is in 'First Fruits style' it has several features which seem to indicate either repair of the old building or borrowing from it. The architect is not known for certain, but John Bowden and John Semple have both been suggested.(12) There are very elegant and unusual clusters of finials at the top of the tower, known elsewhere from around the second half of the eighteenth century, and so probably from the older church on the site, and also more attractive windows than the typical first fruits church.

Ahamlish Church

The cost was £800, of which £100 was donated by Lord Palmerston and £700 was borrowed from the Board of First Fruits. There was no Glebe land at all, and no Glebe House as such,(13) but the Soden family rented Ahamlish House to the rector. They lived at Moneygold at this stage.(14) J.C. Curwen, a traveller in Ireland in 1818, reports that he was told locally that the rector and his family were the only Protestants in the parish of Ahamlish. He noted that the rector of Ahamlish spent a lot of time engaged in the local cottage industry of burning kelp(the stalks of *laminaria digitata*) and went on to say that he could not help expressing a wish that his time could be more appropriately directed.(15) However he had not the possibility of farming Glebe land as other rectors had, and with little or no congregation he must have been hard put to it to make a living. The burning of kelp had not always been encouraged, as it destroyed the spawn beds and so cut down the number of fish.

Ahamlish has been in and out of the Parish of Drumcliffe with regularity. In 1615 they had their own clergyman, but there would have been a pre-Reformation church on the site, as it is an ancient holy place, associated with St. Molaise of Inishmurray- Molaise's well is nearby, and St. Molaise is traditionally believed to have pronounced sentence on St. Columba after the Battle of the Books at the "Cross of Ahamlish".(16) In 1674 Ahamlish again became part of Drumcliffe parish, then it separated again in 1766. In 1968 the church was closed down altogether and was deconsecrated in 1969. But the graveyard is still fully in use, and is the main burying place for the Roman Catholic parish of St. Molaise's in Cliffoney. There are still very old rights of way from Ahamlish graveyard to the river and onto the bog.

Ahamlish House

VICARS OF AHAMLISH

In 1903 Stanley Lane-Poole, who made a study of the 'congested districts' of Ahamlish and Mullaghmore, noted that "The Vicar of Ahamlish drives five miles from Moneygold to read the Church of Ireland service on Sunday afternoons to the few   visitors and coastguards who live in the row of white cottages beyond the flagstaff - English to a man and all 'black protestants' - as a fisherman confided to me, more in humour than in malice".(17) The vicar referred to here would be the Reverend John McCormick, the last vicar of Ahamlish. McCormick was called a vicar rather than a rector because the 'rectory' of Ahamlish was impropriate to Lord Palmerston, which meant that Palmerston owned the tithes, and had the right to choose the incumbent, whom he employed as his representative or vicar.

John McCormick would have seen some changes in Mullaghmore and Ahamlish, but his predecessor the Reverend Charles West, the burner of kelp, would have seen more. West would have seen the Cliffoney Hotel extended and beautified, as Lord Palmerstown lived there while Classiebawn was being built; spending more than the total revenue of the estate on improvements. He would have seen the Cliffoney dispensary built; and best of all the Mullaghmore harbour built in 1822, with money half from the Commission of Fisheries and half from local subscriptions. This harbour was designed by engineer Alexander Nimmo, and was by that time an urgent necessity, as the previous winter eleven of the fourteen fishing boats in the village were wrecked in storms. It was built with local labour, with a two month suspension of work to get in the crops. Two years into his incumbency West had been appointed as one of the special magistrates appointed by the crown to compensate people whose property had been damaged during the 1798 uprising.

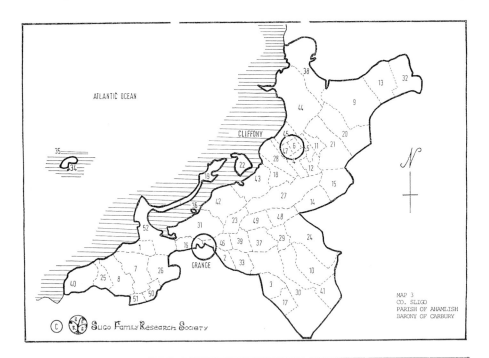

MAP 3
CO. SLIGO
PARISH OF AHAMLISH
BARONY OF CARBURY

MAP 3 CO. SLIGO - PARISH OF AHAMALISH - BARONY OF CARBURY

1	AGHARROW	21	CREEVYMORE	41	LYLE
2	ARDNAGLASS LOWER	22	DERNISH ISLAND	42	MONEYGOLD
3	ARDNAGLASS UPPER	23	DERRY	--	MOUNTEDWARD See 26
4	BALLINCASTLE	24	DERRYLEHAN	43	MOUNT TEMPLE
5	BALLINPHULL	25	DOONSHASKIN	44	MULLAGHMORE
6	BALLYNABROCK	26	DRANGAN OR MOUNTEDWARD	45	MULLAGHMORE WEST
7	BALLYSCANNEL	27	DRUMFAD	46	NEWTOWN
8	BREAGHWY	28	EDENREAGH	47	NEWTOWNCLIFFONY
9	BUNDUFF	29	GORTADERRY	48	RATHFRASK
10	CARROWNAMADDOO	30	GORTNALECK	49	RATHHUGH
11	CARTRONKILLERDOO	31	GRANGE	50	SILVERHILL
12	CARTRONPLANK	32	GRELLAGH	51	SRAREVAGH
13	CASTLEGAL	33	GROGAGH	52	STREEDAGH
14	CASTLEGOWAN	34	ILLAUNATIR ISLAND *		
15	CLOONERCO	35	INISHMURRAY		
16	CLOONTYPROCKLIS	36	INISHNAGOR **		
17	CLOYRAGH	37	KILCAT		
18	CLOYSPARRA	38	KILKILLOGE		
19	CONOR'S ISLAND	39	KILTYKERE		
20	CREEVYKEEL	40	LISLARY		

Parish of Ahamlish - by kind permission of Sligo family Research Society

DRUMCLIFFE - The Church of Ireland Parish in its North Sligo Setting.

PARSON YEATS

The curate the Reverend Edward Ayres, would have been in charge during the vacancy caused by the departure of the Revd Richard Wynne for Annagh (modern Belturbet). Wynne however still served the diocese as Precentor of Elphin cathedral. He became Precentor of St. Patrick's Cathedral Dublin a little later. In 1811 the new rector arrived. He was the former curate, who had been curate to Richard Wynne in 1802, the Revd John Yeats. One wonders if his few hours spent in prison since his curacy, after his friend Robert Emmet's unsuccessful rising, were known to the Drumcliffe parishioners. He was a Trinity College Dublin graduate, and had won a medal for excellence in Greek while there.

Yeats appears to have been a popular figure, and of quite a different nature from the careful Richard Wynne who looked after the money. He seems to have been more casual about such matters, and several times in succession the churchwardens were obliged to call on the rector to try and obtain the money to pay the arrears owing to the painter of the church. Then nine months later it is noted in the vestry book that he owed the parish £9-15-1d.

But on the positive side, in a poem written by his great-grandson, W.B. Yeats, the poet mentions that he re-erected the ancient High Cross, which seemingly had been in some disrepair - maybe even lying abandoned in a corner, as was the broken cross which Walker took away and is now in the National Museum. The parish seems to have enjoyed a period of relative prosperity and good church attendance during his time. Thomas Kerrigan was appointed in 1818 to take care of the horses during Divine Service, and the next year the graveyard was gravelled and an iron gate put in place. It is interesting to note that the monthly elements at this time cost on average three pounds and ten shillings.(18)

The Reverend John Yeats, affectionately known as "Parson Yeats", was the son of a linen-merchant from Dublin, and he married Jane Taylor and they had twelve children, nicely filling the Georgian rectory. Nine of the twelve children were boys and three were girls. A lovely story is told of Parson Yeats. Yeats was going around the parish in company with Sir Robert Gore-Booth's agent Dodwell, and a bailiff, one of the Barbers, and exhorting people to send their children to the Protestant school at Milltown. At one cottage they visited, a man called James O'Hara told him stoutly that no child of his would ever darken the door of that school-house. Yeats commended him for his spirit and told him he was "the honestest man they had come across that day"!(19)

In his book *"Reveries over Childhood and Youth"* his great grandson William Butler Yeats also tells this story, but in his version it is a woman who declares she would not let her child go to the Protestant school, and the parson replies "Thank you my woman, you are the first honest woman I have met today!" The poet also tells how he has been told his ancestor was so kind and anxious not to find out anyone in any fault, that he always advertised his presence whenever he went into the kitchen by loudly rattling his bunch of keys!(20)

The Rectory at Drumcliffe, c.1797 - Photo by kind permission of Fr. John Carroll

THE METAL MAN

It was during Yeats's incumbency that the Metal Man was erected in Rosses Point. In the channel between Oyster Island and Rosses Point there was a rock called the perch rock which was very dangerous and only exposed at half tide. The beacon is topped with a giant metal figure of a sailor who is pointing with his arm to the place where the water is deep enough for ships. Thomas Kirk designed him and Thomas Ham of Ballina is known to have manufactured four, but only this one and the one in Waterford have been traced. The Waterford Metal Man overlooks Tramore Bay on Great Newton Head.

The Sligo Metal Man was erected in 1822, and three years later it was decided he would look better painted up , and so he does, being a figure very popular locally. Legend even has it that at certain times of year he leaves his pedestal and goes ashore for a few pints! Parson Yeats's famous great grandson Jack Yeats painted a lovely picture of Rosses Point called *Memory Harbour*, that evokes very well its atmosphere of pirates and smugglers, and features the Metal Man.

PROBLEM OF THE BLOWN SAND

A local problem which had been going on for a few decades and became greatly aggravated in the 1830's was the phenomenon of blown sand. The area surrounding Maugherow, Raughley and Mullaghmore, was in danger of becoming completely buried and five hundred acres were already under depths of up to ten feet of sand.(21) This was caused by exceptionally high tides pushing the sand further up the shore and then the wind blowing it inland as there was nothing to stop the erosion. Some of the cottages on the coast were buried up to their roofs and the inhabitants were forced to dig their way in through a hole in the thatch.

Three landlords were involved, John Gethin, Sir Robert Gore-Both and Lord Palmerston. Palmerston led the way in the 1820's planting bent grass, *arunda arenarea*, obtained from Russia, and the other two followed. At first they tried, at the cost of £5 per acre, planting the grass. This did not halt the erosion. But the solution was a very simple one - they had planted the bent too neatly aligned in straight rows. When they realised this, they replanted, staggering the plants, and at last the blown sands were halted. Ballintemple was particularly badly hit. Once the bent had stopped the erosion, Robert Stevenson, Palmerston's agent at the time, recommended reclaiming the land with maritime pine, broom and marram grass, and this was done successfully.

FAMINE OF 1822

Parson Yeats must have lived through gruelling times, for in 1822 there was a severe famine and many people died. It is particularly telling, and also rather moving, to read that in 1824 a Coffin Committee had to be appointed in the parish.(22) This famine was followed by a severe cholera epidemic in 1832, and later another period of famine (both earlier than the famous Great Famine in 1845-7). *The Sligo Journal* in 1822 was full of notices of ships sailing to New York and Quebec. Yeats was a burgess of Sligo town, and was himself very active in the work of relief during the early famine, distributing oatmeal among the starving people of Drumcliffe, and procuring a gift of several tons of grain from a generous parishioner.

This famine was less severe than the Great Famine because the grain was plentiful. Yeats was commended for his diligence in *The Sligo Journal*.(23) Together with several gentlemen from the parish of Drumcliffe - Soden, Parke and Wynne - he sat on the Famine Relief Committee, a group of men who were untiring in their exertions to help the starving.

CATHOLIC EMANCIPATION

In 1826 Catholics at last were given the vote, thanks to the dedicated and determined efforts of Daniel O'Connell and the bloodless revolution he effected through the work of The Catholic Association. But Roman Catholics could not sit in Parliament, this old law from penal times was still not revoked. However the wording did not prohibit someone from standing for Parliament. So in 1828 O'Connell stood for the Clare seat in the bye-election, and overwhelmingly defeated Vesey Fitzgerald the Protestant candidate; although of course O'Connell could not take up his seat, being a Roman Catholic. But the blow for freedom had been struck, Wellington and Peel over in Westminster took note, and on 13th. April 1829 Catholic Emancipation became law.

DRUM SCHOOL

In 1826 although Church of Ireland schools were listed in Drumcliffe and Ahamlish, Ahamlish seems to have had no teachers, whereas Drumcliffe seems to have had five - John Jackson of Drum, William Maxwell of Cooladrummin, Jane McKim of Ballinfull, Thomas Gibson of Tully Hill and William Burchart (a dissenter) of Kilsellagh. There were fourteen Roman Catholic teachers in Drumcliffe that same year, and five between Grange and Ahamlish.(24)

In 1831 Parson Yeats was signatory to a 999-year lease of some land in the townland of Drum East, by Owen Wynne of Hazelwood. The lessor was The Society for Promoting The Education Of The Poor In Ireland, and the purpose was for building a school. The rent charged was "a peppercorn annually, if demanded".

The school had two classrooms - the boys' and the girls' - a hall and a teacher's residence attached. It was registered as a state National school in 1880, and continued on until 1913 when it was obliged to close due to the fall in the number of pupils. Complaints of the small number of pupils had been common during its history, also the teaching of religious instruction to non-Church of Ireland pupils. When it closed those pupils remaining were conveyed to Milltown School in a covered van provided jointly by the National Education Commission and the parish.

Drum School was sold to the McCullough family in 1920 and the building was used as a family home and farmhouse for the next sixty years. Old ink bottles were found in the garden, and partitions from between the classrooms were used as ceilings in the recent renovations by Aidan and Dolores McKeown.

The Old Schoolhouse at Drum East

Drum was also a strong Methodist area, and Wesley is reputed to have preached standing on a certain stone in Drum. At Drum Cross there was a combined or 'federal' Methodist and Presbyterian Church, which has also has been converted into a private dwelling. There was also an older Presbyterian Church nearby in Cloonderry townland, which predated the federation, and used to be known locally as "The Four O'Clock", as many people went to services in both churches. In 1895 Drum Methodist Church was the venue for the "Drum Mutual Improvement Association", which was a Temperance movement.

MUNNINANE SCHOOL.

In 1841, Owen Wynne sold a portion of land in the townland of Munninane for the sum of five shillings to the governors of the Erasmus Smith School, so that a school should be built there where the pupils would be instructed in the Holy Scriptures. Some have mentioned another Erasmus Smith School at Lislahelly, but there is no trace of this, and it could be a misunderstanding based on the fact that the trustees owned land at Lislahelly. Erasmus Smith had been a pious Puritan, who was a wealthy London merchant, born in 1611. His father Sir Roger Smith of Leicestershire had given him some land in Ireland during the 1641 rebellion, and Erasmus Smith eventually owned 46,000 acres. He founded five Grammar Schools and five Elementary Schools with the aim of training boys for the ministry and teaching Latin, Greek and Hebrew. The Board which continued the work after his death also endowed King's Hospital School and Trinity College Dublin Library.

To give an idea of the numbers involved, by 1870 the Erasmus Smith School at Munninane had 23 pupils, all Church of Ireland, Ballinphull School near Lissadell had 23 Church of Ireland pupils and eight Presbyterians; Drum had 24 pupils, of which 16 were Presbyterian and only eight Church of Ireland. Milltown had 40 pupils-39 Church of Ireland pupils and one other. There were also Church of Ireland children at National Schools, three at Raughley, (presumably coastguards' children), five at Mullaghmore, six at Rathcormack and six at Carney.(25)

CHOLERA EPIDEMIC

In 1832 another tragedy, the disease cholera, hit the town of Sligo and the countryside around, started off by a visitor from Westport where the disease was rife. But no one wanted the sufferers in their locality, and in their haste to avoid contamination some people affected with the disease were even buried alive. Sligo woman Charlotte Stoker, mother of the novelist Bram Stoker who wrote *Dracula*, regaled her son with stories like these and worse, which must have made a deep impression on him. A local doctor reported that a ruffianly mob armed with clubs protested against the move to convert the fever hospital into a cholera hospital, and to set up Boards of Health in Carney and Ballymote.(26) Observers at the time said that "the green field beside the fever hospital was white with the freshly sawn wood of rows of coffins held in readiness, as the cholera epidemic swept the town and country".(27)

Interestingly enough the figures given show that the sufferers from the Cholera Asiatica had a fifty-per-cent chance of survival if they were left in the country, but those brought into the fever hospital had a less than thirty-per-cent chance of survival. The tragedy was that although many fled from the town to the country, the country folk would not take them in because of the pestilence and many died in the ditches in which they had sought shelter. Three out of four of the doctors assigned to the epidemic succumbed to the disease.

SOCIAL CONDITIONS IN 1837

Jonathan Binns has left us a graphic description of social conditions at this time, taking as typical a family called Waters on Lord Palmerston's estate.(28) Their cabin had no chimney, and only one small window. He paid an annual rent of £1-15s. for his cabin and a rood of ground, on which he would grow potatoes and graze his cow. He paid the priest a shilling a year; the tithes he officially owed the Church of Ireland clergy had not been collected for the last three years. He and his wife would live on the potatoes they grew and the profit from selling pigs and poultry and butter; his wife's spinning would pay the rents and clothing and extra food - they bought one item of clothing every second year 'on tick'.

In spite of their poverty Mr. Waters would lay on a three-day long feast for the neighbours when his daughter married. Palmerston had more tenants than he could afford to employ so each month the names were put into a hat and that month's names would be drawn out. Mr. Waters was richer than average as he had a job breaking stones for the roads. On Captain Jones's estate along the coast at Streedagh the tenants paid at least half their annual rent from the sale of sea-weed for fertilizer - although agent Dodwell disapproved of this practice, saying it was a forcer and an exhauster.(29)

Emigration had already begun at this stage, and Matthew Barber of Carney and the Ferguson family of Drumcliffe had emigrated to America as early as 1815, together with several Roman Catholic families from Grange, Magherow and Mount Temple.(30)

DEATH OF PARSON YEATS

Towards the end of Yeats's ministry in Drumcliffe, there were several big changes in the administration of the Church of Ireland. One was the passing of The Tithe Act in 1838, so that now the tithes were part of the rent and were collected by the landlord; this was aimed to put a stop to The Tithe Wars which were happening in some parts of the country. The other was the passing of the Church Temporalities Act in 1841, which meant that there were no longer four Archiepiscopal Provinces - Armagh, Dublin, Cashel and Tuam - but only two, Armagh and Dublin. Dr. John Leslie, the Bishop of Elphin, a cousin of the Duke of Wellington, became Bishop of the united dioceses that year, and continued on until his death in 1854, aged 82. The Diocese of Elphin now no longer came under Tuam, but went to Armagh Province and was united with Kilmore and Ardagh Diocese. Ardagh had been united to Kilmore a few years previously, in 1839. 1839 was the year of the Big Wind, an almost tornado-like gale which did considerable damage to Lissadell and to Haslewood, felling a thousand trees at Haslewood and reducing some cottages to heaps of rubble.

"Parson Yeats" had a succession of curates, including Charles Dunne, George Vaughan Hart, and Edward Lloyd Elwood, the last of whom married Yeats's daughter Eleanor (Ellen). His son Thomas Yeats also served as church-warden in Drumcliffe for a time. Towards the end of his ministry Parson Yeats saw the Drumcliffe floodlands drained, which no doubt would have given him much pleasure, and part of the project was the construction of weirs to supply water to the Collinsford Mill and the Drumcliffe Corn Mill.

In his excellent biography of the poet William Butler Yeats, talking of Parson Yeats, Stephen Coote says: "It was only on his death in 1846 that it was dis-covered how this good man had had a relish for the pleasures of life which extended to his building a secret liquor cupboard in his Drumcliffe Rectory and stocking it at the cost of £400 in credit. Revd. William Butler Yeats promptly paid his father's debts".(31)

Fort Louis

Yeats died in 1846, at the start of the Great Famine. His wife Jane had died four years previously. Four of their twelve children stayed on in the county. Matthew lived at Fort Louis in Rathbraughan (also known as Rathbraughan Cottage), a charming mid-eighteenth century house built by Colonel Gubbins who had fought in the American War of Independence - hence the name. It was originally built as a shooting lodge, in the early eighteenth century, and the front part was added on in the late eighteenth century. Matthew was a land-agent with a family of six, and W.B.Yeats remembers sailing boats with his children in the little river in the grounds.(32) Matthew acted as a synodsman for Drumcliffe parish for many years.

Thomas gave up a promising career as a mathematician to look after his sister Mickey. Mickey was unmarried and seems to have been a farmer. She lived in the creeper covered two storied farmhouse with box borders at Cregg, called Seaview. This house had once been used as the Rectory of Drumcliffe before the building of the big Georgian rectory. The eldest son, the Revd William Butler, was the father of John Butler Yeats the artist, and thus grandfather of the poet W.B.Yeats. He followed his father into holy orders, ministering at Tullylish near Portadown in Co. Armagh. While at Trinity College Dublin this tall redheaded young man, a friend of Isaac Butt founder of the Home Rule Movement, was deemed the best jockey of his day.

IMPROVING THE LAND-THE PRE-FAMINE YEARS

Palmerston instituted many other improvements besides the building and planting already noted. He drained bog areas with gravel and applied lime and seaweed, and he abolished on his estate the 'rundale' method of farming whereby farms were divided up between families into smaller and smaller holdings. The Gore-Booths and other families were hard at work trying to improve

Rahelly House - By kind permission of the Revd. Noel Regan

their estates at this time. In particular Francis Barber, a tenant of the Gore-Booths who rented a large acreage, worked very hard draining the land, spending almost £20,000 on the project. He built a large house, Rahelly, in Neo-Tudor style with a fine courtyard and a bell tower, and hood mouldings over the windows - a feature of many Sligo houses, sometimes referred to as 'eyebrows'

This success story ended sadly however, as Barber's engineering works in Sligo town landed him into considerable financial difficulty. He was building a sewage system for the town and was obliged to settle claims made by people who sustained damage to their property owing to the blasting through rock that was necessary to make the sewage system. He mortgaged Rahelly to the Gore-Booths to pay his debts, and the family were never able to buy it back. During the Civil War the house was occupied by troops of both sides at different times, finally being burnt by Free State troops in 1923.

Sir Robert Gore-Booth's father had been largely an absentee landlord, but Sir Robert instigated many improvements with the help of his agent, Dodwell. He aided 262 people to emigrate at a cost to him of four pounds each, from the very poor townland of Ballygilgan. He offered each tenant either their fare to Canada, or an equivalent amount of land in Rossinver parish, the object being to place people on farms which were of manageable size rather than just the tiny small-holdings which had been created by the unfortunate laws of succession in Penal times.(33)

He paid the fare of Parson Yeats's son Richard so that he could help the other passengers in their search for work when they reached St. John, and he also had an agent in St. John organised to look after them, John Robertson. Richard Yeats was pleasant and agreeable to all, and took two services on deck every Sunday, not omitting a sermon. One of Lady Gore-Booth's contributions to the general improvements on the estate had been to offer a prize of a free cow for the best kept cottage and she also gave a cow to the ship *The Yeoman of Greenock*, which was a great help for the children; while the fiddler on board kept everyone happy.(34)

PART VII:
THE GREAT FAMINE AND
THE LATER NINETEENTH CENTURY

THE FAMINE OF 1845-1847

The famine started with the partial failure of the potato crop in 1845 owing to blight. Then in 1846 there were food riots and severe unemployment, followed by failure of the potato crop, the potatoes melting into a smelly mush. The rural population was harder struck than the townspeople and death by starvation became common, the district coroner arriving at Magherow one day to certify a row of forty corpses. Soup kitchens were opened by private individuals, and help was sent from Dublin eventually. Sir Robert Gore-Booth mortgaged Lissadell for £50,000, and also sold some of his property in England to help his tenants. He brought bread and oatmeal to the starving on a cart and when he fell ill Lady Gore-Booth distributed the food for nine hours in constant hail and cold. The Reverend William Jeffcott the Lissadell curate at the time also played a major part in organising relief. (The ecclesiastical status of the Lissadell clergy was perpetual curates, Francis Hassard was the curate of Drumcliffe).

In 1847 fever broke out and the water supply was found to be contaminated. To cap it all the cholera broke out again, and this too was more severe in country regions, especially the Doonfore area. Drumcliffe too was badly hit, and Ahamlish suffered particularly badly, with only 700 people employed out of a total of 10,000, and the workhouse full to bursting with 1,227 inmates and the doors, of necessity, closed to more. Lord Palmerston was largely an absentee, his estates being managed by the firm of Stewart and Kincaid, who did try to help people but rather late in the day.

As well as starvation and fever, unemployment was a problem, and schemes to create employment were created, as well as Relief Commissions being set up. During Peel's Tory government people did reasonably well, the government arranging the sending of Indian corn and meal from America, but the new Whig administration would not allow any interference with private enterprise, and the government stores were very meanly managed; the tragedy and the scandal lay here as much as anywhere.

There was a steady stream of emigration which effectively reduced the population of County Sligo to considerably less than two-thirds its previous level, the Sligo population decreasing by fifty-nine and a quarter thousand over the ten year period. But, as the *Sligo Champion* reported, the emigrants tended to be of the better classes, not the truly needy.(1) By 1847 13,000 people had emigrated, 203 miles of road had been built, 106 miles of roads had been repaired, the sewerage system built, the workhouse enlarged to allow a further 500 people in, and the infirmary enlarged - great work, but gruelling to do it with nothing but boiled cabbage in your stomach. By the end of the Famine years the Poor Law

Guardians owed the Provincial Bank £16,000. James Barber of Carney was a Poor Law Guardian, and he oversaw the fever hospital which opened in Carney at the time.

THOMAS CRAWFORD'S INCUMBENCY

After his death in 1847 Yeats was succeeded as Rector of Drumcliffe by the Reverend Thomas Crawford, who also served until his death, in 1871.(2) He it was who gave permission for Rosses Point to be severed from the mother parish to form a new parochial district, and the first stone was laid in 1854. See the section on this further on. Two years later the foundation stone of Lissadell Church was laid by Hannah Lady Gore-Booth, Sir Robert's mother.

Crawford cared for the parish during the most difficult time of what is generally now known as The Great Famine. There were earlier famines, and also a later famine; but here in the North-West the 1845-1847 famine was particularly bad and would merit the prefix. (I add this as revisionism is fashionable, especially in Dublin, which was not so badly hit). During this time help was poured into the county and parish, including a grant for £3,000 from the Mansion House Committee for the Relief of Distress in Ireland, for cooperating with the Fisheries Board in the building of a harbour at Raughley. Like Mullaghmore harbour, this too was designed by Alexander Nimmo, who was civil engineer to the Irish government, and was appointed as manager of works designed to employ the people of Mayo, Sligo and Galway.

During Crawford's time the windows were fitted with panes of three different colours of glass in their top sections, which are still in place today. His wife Mrs. Crawford paid for six of these, Miss Eleanor Crawford for one and Lady Gore-Booth for one. At this time the Glebe land of Drumcliffe comprised 70 acres, and was worth £80. The Rector's stipend was £270 per annum, with no augmentations. His curate was the Reverend John Finnerty.

A sadness during Crawford's time at Drumcliffe was the death of his young wife in 1860, aged only 29, and also his daughter Emma. He died in 1871 and is buried with them in the graveyard. Crawford served under three different bishops of Kilmore. One of these, Bishop Hamilton Verscoyle of the Donegal family of Dutch extraction, was consecrated to Kilmore in 1862, having previously filled the posts of both Chancellor of Christchurch Cathedral and Dean of Ferns. He was a studious bishop and a distinguished figure in the House of Lords, and his sermons were published under the title "The Bond of Perfectness".(3)

An excitement during Thomas Crawford's incumbency was the discovery in 1867 of two wounded men on the beach at Streedagh, who had been landed by "a Brigantine of very suspicious appearance".(4) They were found by the chief boatman in charge of the Streedagh Coastguard Station. These were later discovered to have been part of a planned Fenian invasion of Ireland from America. The Brigantine was full of arms, and a revolver exploded accidentally wounding the two men. The invasion was cancelled by local agents.(5).

There were flourishing coastguard stations also at Raughley (six men), Rosses Point (eight men) and Mullaghmore (nine men).The Raughley coastguards were particularly active, with the wreck of *The Rose* off Ardboline island in 1867 and later the *Sligo II* in the same place in 1912.(6)

Rosses Point Church

NEW CHURCH AT ROSSES POINT

For the four years from 1854 to 1858 the new Church at Rosses Point was being built. It was a small limestone church with a small spire capping the tower in proportion to the size of the building. The architect was William Dean Butler.

Previously it had always been part of Drumcliffe parish. Mrs. Cooper of Markree castle whose family owned Elsinore at the time, used to have summer services in her house at Elsinore, gathering together an impromptu congregation; and whichever clergyman was holidaying at Rosses Point at the time would conduct the service. As the number of Protestant visitors seemed always to be on the increase, an arrangement was made to create a separate parochial district and build Rosses Point church. The church cost £500, and was looked after for the first eleven years by the rector of Drumcliffe until they eventually had their own incumbent, the Reverend Frederick Flood, in 1869. Rosses Point church went back to Drumcliffe group of parishes for a while in the early 1930's, and the Rectory was renamed Joppa Lodge, and used for clergy families to have holidays in exchange for light duties; it has been sold now, but Church Cottage nearby is used for the same purpose, thus keeping up the tradition of visiting clergy taking the services in the summer. Today the parish is looked after by the Dean of

Elphin, who has the Cathedral Church of St. John in Sligo and St. Anne's, Knocknarea as well.

During this time, in 1855, there was a very severe winter with what was known as "The Great Freeze", and people were able to skate on Lough Gill for a third of its area for a fortnight. Many plants were injured or killed at that time.

Lissadell Church

LISSADELL CHURCH

After the Famine people expressed gratitude to Sir Robert Gore-Booth, John Arthur Wynne and other landowners and farmers who had done what they could to help. When Sir Robert stood for election to Parliament, a campaign was stirred up to discredit him. Apparently this was the order of the day in these elections. Gore-Booth's efforts during the famine were passed over, and facts about his earlier clearance of Ballygilgan were falsified, even including accusations that a ship, *The Pomona*, sunk with all its passengers. Retired county librarian and indefatigable local historian John McTernan has obtained assurance from the National Maritime Museum that *The Pomona*, under her Captain, Master Doyle, did reach her destination, and even made several other voyages thereafter.(7)

From study of the family papers of the landlords together with local enquiries, a picture seems to emerge of the landlords believing they were acting very magnanimously and charging low rents, while the agents were very unpopular and probably not putting into effect the exact instructions of their bosses. Memories of the unpopularity of the Gore-Booths' agent Dodwell and the Wynnes' agent Olpherts, are still very much alive locally.

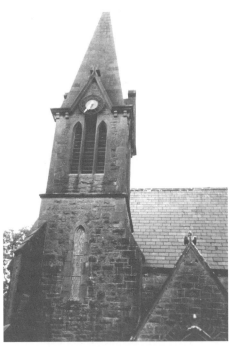

Lissadell Church Tower

Lissadell Church, started in 1856, replaced a chapel of ease built by Sir Robert Gore-Booth probably in 1842, which was when the Reverend William Jeffcott arrived. The new church was built behind this chapel-of-ease, which stood where the gravelled carpark is now in front of the church. The church was probably designed by J.Wellend.(8) It is a fine Gothic style building with a pyramidal capped tower with gablets, in rusticated limestone, and it has a clock in the tower, presented by tenants of the Lissadell estate in memory of Sir Robert. This clock has recently been restored by Dr. Jim Gibson in memory of his wife Muriel, nee Siggins.

There are some fine stained glass windows. The oldest window is the west window, in memory of Hannah Gore-Booth, mother of Sir Robert, who laid the foundation stone. According to the Reverend Arthur Cotter, the last Rector of Lissadell, who had been chaplain to the British Embassy in Paris, the rose window above it is a copy of one in Paris. The east window is in memory of Caroline Susan Gore-Booth, Sir Robert's wife, by William Warrington of London, dated 1857. Another two, "Harmonia" and Fortitudo" are fine pieces by Irish stained glass artist Ethel Rhind, two of her earliest, and unsigned.(9) They are dated 1907, the year before she joined the *An Tur Gloine* studio, (the Tower of Glass). They are in memory of Augusta Gore-Booth, known as 'wee Ga' because of her small height, who used to play the organ in the church. It is said of her that she learned to play the violin while flat on her back recovering from a riding accident. The organ is made by Wheildon of Manchester, and has a fine mahogany case. The adjacent two windows are by Kitty O'Brien and are in memory of two brothers, Brian and Hugh Gore-Booth, who were killed during the Second World War - details of that are further on.

The new church was consecrated on 4th. June 1858. Bishop Beresford preached on the text "How dreadful is this place.......this is none other than the House of God." It was the sixth new church he had consecrated in Elphin Diocese since his appointment four years earlier.(10)

There is also a rusticated limestone schoolhouse to match the church, with a high-pitched roof and pierced barge-boarding, just across the road, with a teacher's residence attached. The Glebe House is further down the road, built in

Lissadell Glebe House

the same stone, in a Tudor style, with many chimneys. A story attaches to this building, told by Jim Barber. Jim's grandfather was asked to build the house, but when he dug for the foundations he found it was a bog; and the deeper he dug the more boggy it seemed to be. He reported this to his employer, who told him to build it there anyway. So he cut down some oak trees and made a raft of their trunks to form a foundation for the house, and it has survived intact to this day!(11)

Lissadell School House

LOCAL FAMILIES

It is interesting to find that many names in the nineteenth century church registers are identical to the names found today. The Barbers were then - as now - the most numerous family, and were found in Carney, Rahelly and Barnaribbon as well as Coonmel; there were Hunters at Keelty, Meldrums at Milltown, Warrens at Carney, Lindsays at both Munninane and Tully, Shaws at Ballinagalliagh, and Greggs at Bunavalley, Henrys at Lissadell, Walkers at Ballinfull, Shaws at Ballinavolagh, Clarkes at Ballinvogher, Andersons at Drum, and Gore-Booths at Lissadell. Other names which occurred frequently were Frizelle, Kerr and Regan. The Cunningham family were also quite numerous. Five Cunningham brothers from Ayr in Scotland had settled in the Drum area, the five belonging to four different religious denominations.

Names which appear a lot in the vestry lists were those of Parke of Dunally, the Jones's of Cregg House, and the Gore-Booth family. There were also Jones's at Mt. Edward and Springfield and the Ormsby-Jones's at Streedagh House, and the Gore-Jones family had houses at Johnsport and Raughley. John Gore-Jones senior was a Resident Magistrate, and his son John was editor of *The Sligo Journal* for a number of years in the 1850's. The first member of the Parke family, Roger, came over from Kent in 1601 with Sir Roger Jones, and Dunally Castle was his residence, which had previously been an O'Donnell fortress. His younger sons inherited it while his elder son Captain Roger Parke built the fortified house already referred to in Part IV, on the northern shore of Lough Gill, called Newtown Manor, incorporating an earlier castle there which had belonged to the O'Rourkes. It is now known as Parke's Castle, and is well-restored and worth a visit.

In the nineteenth century the Dunally Parkes were involved in a lengthy legal wrangle between two relatives over land; and also about the proposed Enniskillen to Sligo railway (or rather the Sligo extension of the already existing Enniskillen to Bundoran Railway) which was to have been routed through their land. They claimed and were awarded the handsome compensation of £225 but the railway was never built. The land was actually owned by Viscount Palmerston. Parke was the lessor and occupier.

Lt. Col Sir William Parke in 1837 on his retirement from active service in the army, which he served in the West Indies, Egypt, Gibralter and the Iberian peninsula, became a magistrate, High Sheriff for a while, and Deputy Lieutenant. He was a moderate in politics, and the leader of the liberal faction, and created quite a sensation locally when he got together a jury composed mostly of Roman Catholics, all his fellow members of the Liberal Club, and only one Protestant. The Assize Judge fined him £10 for this, as it was contrary to statute!

Another family who played a part in local affairs, as well as the Parke family, and the Jones family of Cregg House, both of whom have already been mentioned, were the Gethins. The Gethin family owned land locally, but their main residence was Ballindoon on Lough Arrow. Percy Gethin the artist born in

DRUMCLIFFE - The Church of Ireland Parish in its North Sligo Setting.

88

1874, who died in the First World War, was from the Holywell branch of the family. Simpson of Millbrook and Slade of Mount Shannon are two families also mentioned in Lewis's *Topographical Dictionary.*

The *Parliamentary Gazetteer* of 1846 also lists amongst the houses of notable size, some of which are still familiar - Elsinore, Mt. Edward, Springfield, Tully, Oxfield, Millbrook, Washington and Summerhill. In the early nineteenth century the petty sessions courts used to take place at Summerhill, and the manor court at Ardtermon.

The church records show that the main occupation was farming, with a sprinkling of trades such as shoemaker, tanner, carpenter, gardener, soldier, lighthouse keeper, police constable and coastguard.

SOME NOTABLE HOUSES

Cregg House and Kildonagh House (formerly known as Ballincar House) must have been built by the same builder, in a typically Sligo style of the eighteenth century, with a porch with a door in the side, and hood mouldings over the windows. Cregg House has seen many occupants - the Nicholsons, Jones's, Hillasses, Smithwicks, Gethins, the Hon. J. King, and then in the nineteenth century Captain Alex Lumsden, an active member of the Drumcliffe vestry, and in 1822 Edward Henderson who let it out for the bathing season. It is now the home of the sisters of the La Sagesse Order who have been running a school and home for the mentally handicapped in the grounds since 1955.

Ballincar Castle is a T-shaped rubble-built seventeenth century stronghouse with double diagonal chimney-pots and small angled windows for defence.(12)

Left: Cregg House before alterations - Photo by Kind permission of Helen Kerrin   *Right: Kildonagh House*

Urlar House

Urlar House, in a similar style to Cregg and Kildonagh, was the home of Dr. William Hamilton, who was the dispensary doctor at Carney from 1837-1867 and had the job of inspecting those emigrating both before and after the famine, and emigrated himself in 1867. Later the Somerville family lived at Urlar. Both families played a prominent part in parish affairs.

Mount Shannon House, just over the border of the parish in Shannon Eighter townland, was the nineteenth century home of H.H. Slade, and then of Francis Montgomery Olpherts, a church-warden of Drumcliffe. Olpherts was descended from a Dutch General, Wybrantz Olphertzen, who was granted land in Donegal by King Charles II. He became the agent for the Haslewood Estate, and married Marianna Wynne of Ardaghowen.

Mount Shannon House

Also living in the Olpherts household at Mount Shannon was Eily, a marvellous whistler, so good in fact that she whistled for the Kaiser! Mount Shannon was a Wynne house.

Summerhill House

Summerhill House was built by the Anderson family, later lived in by the Allens, a parish family, the Irwins, the Rowlettes(a Methodist family) and a Presbyterian family the Donagheys who own it today and have a popular pitch and putt course and golf driving range on their land. Like Fort Louis and the almost next door Auburn House (now Lisnalurg House), it has a curved bow in the front, with a little conical roof on top of it. Moorfield in Cullaghbeg is another old house, once the home of Jeremiah Rogers, a steward of the Gore-Booth estate.

Streedagh House

Streedagh House built by the Jones family, is a late eighteenth century two storey house, with a fortified farmyard with pistol loops. Ardeevin is a pleasant long one storey house, in Ballincar, dating from the eighteenth century, which was a dower house of the Gore-Booths. To this day the locals know that road as "Lady Gore's Hill". There is a trace still seen in the field of a footpath from Ardeevin to Auburn House.

Auburn was owned from 1899 by the L'Estrange family, given them as wedding present by Owen Wynne, Evelyn L'Estrange's father; the house had been a steward's house for the Wynne estate. Georgina Lady Gore-Booth, widow of Sir Henry, lived at Ardeevin with her granddaughter Maeve de Markievicz whom she was bringing up. Maeve and her cousin

Auburn House

Stella L'Estrange (Sr.) shared a governess, and so there was much toing and froing between the two houses. Auburn dates from the seventeenth century and is now known as Lisnalurg House. Drumcliffe church warden George Dodwell lived there at one time.

Madeline Wynne also lived at Ardeevin with 'Aunt Gina'. She was an unmarried sister of Evelyn L'Estrange. Mary L'Estrange, the last of that generation, remembers going along the path to help her Aunt Madeline lick envelopes, as Madeline was secretary of the Feis Ceoil. Ardtermon House belonged to the Jones-Henrys, and was gradually added to as time went on, for a long while it was, in common with Fort Louis and several other Sligo houses, one storey in front, and two storey behind.

A charming and unusual cottage, built by the Gethins, one storey but with a basement or a second storey in the back down the hill, with curved bows and a portico, was in the townland of Rathbraughan. Mabel Gethin has lived there within

Cottage at Rathbraughan - Coutesy of Kitty McConkey

living memory, then a retired sea-captain, Captain Coulthard, who bought it as he could see the ships coming into harbour from it, and would be able to fraternise with his fellow seafarers.(13) Judge Flattery and then the Foley family lived there subsequently. It has now been demolished to make way for a housing estate.

DISESTABLISHMENT

The Revd Julius Henry Griffith succeeded Crawford as rector in 1870.(14) Griffith had been a curate not far away at Lurganboy Co. Leitrim, and afterwards moved on to be curate of St. Michael's Limerick, and then rector of Drumcliffe - but this time not Co. Sligo, but the Drumcliffe in the Diocese of Killaloe. During Griffith's incumbency the Church of Ireland was disestablished by act of parliament. At midnight on 31st. December 1870 the Church of Ireland ceased to be the official State church established by law.

The Church of Ireland was becoming more streamlined and efficient, and also financially self sufficient. At the Union in 1800 compensation money was paid to the Church of Ireland for the Liberties and Corporations previously owned by it, and this was paid to the Board of First Fruits. The Board - renamed the Ecclesiastical Commissioners - also gained a lot of extra money from the cutting down of the number of bishoprics in 1833, as there had been a number of very richly endowed bishoprics. Now the hated tithes had gone, and each parish had to pay an assessed "Sustentation" towards the stipend of its clergy and the running of the church, through the Representative Church Body - a new name for the Ecclesiastical Commissioners.

In accordance with the Act, four gentlemen were to be elected in each parish to assume the management and discipline of the parish. So Sir Roger Parke, Matthew Allison, Jeremiah Rogers and Mr. Smith Shaw of Ballynagalliagh were chosen (Drumcliffe had four such administrators, because the proportion had to be two men to one clergyman, and Griffith had a curate, Samuel Adams). Apart from this, the only other change that Disestablishment seems to have made in the day-to-day running of the parish, was a general feeling that all should financially contribute more generously to its upkeep, and a greater zeal in collecting such funds.

A NEW DEMOCRATIC SPIRIT

That same year, in May, there was a curious meeting - chaired not by the clergy but by Roger Clarke - of sixty parishioners, who expressed their willingness to keep the church in repair and provide the sacramental elements. They became rather bold in the absence of the clergy and indulged in a little theological polemic! They expressed their entire approval of the "faithful and manly protest put forward by the evangelical clergy of Dublin" and their "disapproval of the subtle and insidious teaching of ritualistic doctrines which have been introduced there; they deeply regret that they have not been honestly and openly, condemned by the Archbishop of Dublin". The motion that they should "tender the right hand of friendship to their dissenting brethren and that only the pure truths of the gospel as settled at the Reformation should be preached" (15) was passed unanimously.

Another expression of the new democratic spirit of the post disestablishment church was that they decided to dispense with the services of the parish clerk. This was a paid post, and the clerk kept the registers and took some part of the services. The clerk at this time was no longer Thomas Gibson the schoolmaster, but Richard Davis. There seems to have been some strong feeling on the subject as the wording of the vestry resolution is quaintly and unusually forthright:

" Resolved that we consider the services of a clerk in any church as useless and a remnant of barbarism and leading to coldness and apathy in a congregation, and in this church in particular with the finances in such a state as they have been brought unto, we cannot guarantee, nor do we sanction that any monies be appropriated for the purpose. Passed unanimously".(16) Things do not appear to be very happy at this stage of the parish's history. For two years later only six people turned up for the vestry meeting; the incumbent resigned the treasurership of the parish in 1877, then later the same year he resigned altogether and went off to be curate of St. Michael's Limerick. O'Rourke describes him as "a somewhat bellicose gentleman who figured in Petty Sessions Courts oftener, perhaps, than was desirable".(17)

A SUCCESSION OF RECTORS

The Reverend John Guthrie was the next rector(18), and he was appointed by the novel method of an election, which was held in Boyle for some now obscure reason. He stayed in Drumcliffe for only two years, then he left to go over to London and become chaplain of the Thames Mission. The only drama during

Guthrie's incumbency was that the vestry tried without much success to sack the sexton, but this gentleman barricaded himself into his house, and when he finally gave up the house, (having by now been paid his arrears of salary), he made off with a few items of furniture, a table and a clothes horse from the vestry room!

Sexton's House at Drumcliffe

Next came the Revd James Alan French(19), arriving in 1879 straight from his curacy at St. John's Sligo, where he had also been chaplain to the local lunatic asylum. French was a literary man, having been assistant librarian at Trinity College Dublin for four years, and author of *YMCA Lectures* and *Poems*. He was also an accomplished archaeologist, and it was he who told Wood-Martin how to decipher the ogham stone he had found embedded in the wall of the church on Church Island, Lough Gill.

They were dramatic times. In 1879 after a very wet summer the potato crop failed again, almost in its entirety. The rains continued on in Autumn and flooding was serious, and many peoples' supply of turf was ruined. Distress was great, particularly in Magherow, Lissadell and Inishmurray. A relief steamer sent to bring supplies to Inishmurray had great difficulty docking, but eventually managed to land the food. Emigration was on the increase again, not surprisingly. This famine, the fourth famine recorded in the nineteenth century, led to the formation the following year of the Land League by Michael Davitt. This acted as a court to fix fair rents, and helped work towards tenants' ownership of the land, which came gradually with the Land Act and the formation of the Land Commission in 1881 and subsequent Acts leading in 1885 to a system of state aided land purchase. At this period, the local papers record Sir Henry Gore-Booth giving a great 'Harvest Home' meal for three hundred people, regardless of denomination. The local priest was one of the carvers of the joints at this meal.

In 1882 a violent storm wrecked the roof of the Magherow 'chapel' (Roman Catholic churches used to be called chapels in Ireland), injuring several people and killing one. The Gore-Booths helped. It was their custom always to try to give to Roman Catholic and Protestant charities equally. John McTernan has a lovely account in his book "Olde Sligoe" of the oyster pirates, men from Coney Island, Rosses Point and Ballysadare who at this date came to steal the oysters at Lissadell but were met - on two consecutive days - by a flotilla of small boats containing men armed with scythes and hayforks and determined to defend Gore-Booth's oysterbeds.(20)

But the great parish drama during the incumbency of the Revd James Alan French was the terrific storm of 1884, when the capstone of one of the pinnacles of the church tower was blown down and crashed through the roof, smashing slates, rafters and the ceiling, and doing a lot of damage. Apparently whole groves of trees were torn up by the roots. It was fortunate that no-one was hurt. The repair of all this damage took time as well as money and was not completed until the next incumbency in 1895. But things were more stable in the parish now, and money was less of a problem than it had been, since "lady-collectors" had been appointed to go out and collect subscriptions from people, and were doing so very successfully.

COMMUNITY LIFE

Another event during James French's incumbency was the formation of a Drumcliffe Gaelic Athletic Association in 1888 . Its activities were wide ranging and included football, camogie, hurling, figure dancing, gaelic football, ballad singing, butter making awards, and cycling. Handball was also played behind the mill at Milltown (beside the creamery). The butter-making is not surprising as the district was a rich creamery area, and an anonymous writer in 1883 said of Drumcliffe farmers "Their golden butter is fit for a demi-God"!(21) The Drumcliffe Creamery Co-operative was inaugurated in May 1895. *The Irish Homestead* magazine, official newsletter of the Co-operative Movement, reported in May that Josslyn Gore-Booth had worked hard to 'spread the light' among his neighbours and Milltown schoolhouse was full to overflowing at the inaugural meeting. The Revds Ardill and Le Fanu(Lissadell) were on the committee, and two Father Nearys, Catholic curates, were as well, and other familiar names, such as Somerville, Barber, Warren and Henry. A special report came from Sligo by "wire" (nineteenth century name for a telegram) just before the magazine went to print, to say "Agricultural Co-operation has taken the county by storm"! By the end of October the foundation stone of the new creamery had been laid, and two years later the Ballinfull Creamery was opened.

During the 1880's Raughley was starting to rival and even overtake Mullaghmore as the main Sligo fishing port, and it provided a pilot for ships entering Sligo harbour. There was an Annual Regatta at Mullaghmore which had become a popular seaside resort, with apartments known as "The Lodges", which were for rent for a certain sum per month, stables extra. There were Church of Ireland services held there during the Summer at the school, which was then above the Pier Head Hotel. In 1992 these services in the school for holidaymakers were restarted by lay reader Noel Regan of Ballintrillick, now the Reverend Noel Regan.

In those days there was a village shop at Drumcliffe, Cunningham's, and various Church of Ireland folk are noted down in the ledgers as having been regular customers - Mrs. Jinks, The Revd McArdle, The Revd A. French, and the Barbers, Cunninghams, Frizelles, Warrens, Gilmores, McGees, Henrys and Wallaces. An ounce of tobacco back in 1890 cost three pence farthing ! The shop was where the present day surgery - Drumcliffe Family Practice - stands. The shop was also the Drumcliffe Post Office for many years, and the post of postmistress has been filled by a female member of the Cunningham family for four generations, and is still run by descendants in its new site next to the Rectory. Ballinfull post office and shop, beside Lissadell Church, also had one family, the McKims, looking after it for several generations of the McKim family over 60 years. In his book "The Worthies of Sligo" John McTernan reports that two of Drumcliffe's sons in the late nineteenth century became well-known in their professions, Charles Reade the writer, born in Kilsellagh House, Dunally; and Dr. Robert Rowlette, born at Carncash, who became a Professor of Medicine at Trinity College Dublin.(22)

THE REVEREND JOHN ROCHE ARDILL

The penultimate rector of the nineteenth century was a man whose name may still be remembered by some, the Revd John Roche Ardill.(23) He was a scholarly man, trained in the law as well as in theology, the son of a Tipperary landowner. He arrived in the parish from his curacy in St. Andrew's church Dublin, where he was greatly appreciated. The parishioners of St. Andrews presented him with an illuminated address, praising his kindness and zeal in parish work and mentioning that they found his preaching "pure and simple, to the purpose, and attended with great blessing". He spent ten years in the parish, from 1889 to 1899. He wrote three erudite books, *Forgotten Facts of Irish History, St. Patrick* and *The Date of St. Patrick.*

Forgotten Facts of Irish History is a salutary book for anyone to read on the subject of sectarianism and Irish history. He draws his readers' attention to the fact that it was the only English Pope, Pope Adrian IV (Nicholas Breakspear) who 'gave' Ireland to King Henry II of England. Since Pope Urban II's day the papacy had claimed ownership of all Christian islands, and this was later confirmed by Pope Alexander III in 1172.(24) Ardill also reminded his readers that the unpopular Kilkenny Statutes of 1367 prohibiting the Irish language and dress and banning commerce between the English and the Irish were drawn up by Roman Catholic divines(25), and that the tithe laws too were drawn up by the four Roman Catholic archbishops before the Reformation(26).

Ardill's books on St. Patrick were particularly controversial as he suggested that Patrick came to Ireland not in 432 as generally supposed, but as early as 180. He based his hypothesis on the very reasonable grounds of Patrick's appearing to know nothing at all about the Pelagian controversy, which we know was strong throughout Ireland in the fifth century; his not using the Nicene Creed; his bad Latin; his introduction to Ireland of a much simpler and older form of Christianity, with a different date for Easter than the Roman one and a practice of consecrating bishops by only one bishop, not two or more.(27)

During Ardill's incumbency, in 1893, there was a meeting to consider the Church of Ireland petition against Home Rule. The petition was unanimously adopted and £1 sent to aid the Representative Church Body in opposing the measure.(28)

RENOVATIONS TO THE CHURCH

In 1895 the vestry of Drumcliffe decided to have the church plastered with cement mortar by Mark Sweeney and John Monds. This and the other post storm renovations were completed by early autumn and the church was reopened on Sunday the 6th October 1895. The pulpit was moved to the side, and the East wall was decorated. Messrs Meldrum did the job and specially employed Mr.R.L.Clarke to paint the east wall in a "suitable and artistic design".(29) A new school was also built during Ardill's time at Milltown. An organ fund had been started five years previously, and the harmonium had been sold in aid of buying a new organ. Happily this expense was not necessary, as Mr. Ardill obtained in 1890 a good second-hand Dublin made Telford and Telford organ dated 1870 from Powerscourt church as Powerscourt Vestry were buying a larger one.

The event of the Rededication of the church in October 1895 was report-ed by *The Ecclesiastical Gazette* - forerunner of the present day *Church of Ireland Gazette*. The local newspapers had no coverage of the event as they were all at the time completely taken up with reporting the mobs and riots in the streets of Sligo caused by the "Protestant Street Preachers". These men would preach in the streets of Sligo on Sunday afternoons, and the local reaction was somewhat violent. The papers report that an effigy of the Reverend Harrison was burnt in the street by a mob.(30)

Organ at Drumcliffe Church

Milltown School teachers' residence

PART VIII:
THE FIRST HALF OF THE TWENTIETH CENTURY

LIFE IN THE EARLY TWENTIETH CENTURY

Social life centred on church, and on the fairs at Grange, Carney and Magherow held each month, with plenty of celebrations afterwards. Informal gatherings in each others homes were common then as well, with music and dancing. The dances were of the same type as those met with at a 'Ceili' today, such as *The Siege of Ennis, The Stack of Barley* and *The Bridge of Athlone,* in cottages, danced to the music of fiddles and accordions, all played by ear. Many cottages would have had a hollow hearthstone in front of the fire to make the tapping of the feet louder.

In the summer people would gather at the crossroads to play pitch and toss or marbles, and dancing boards were often placed in fields at crossroads. There was horse-racing at Streedagh and Bowmore Strands, and Regattas at Mullaghmore and Raughley. There were lacemaking schools in Cliffoney and Grange. The lace made was the Clones style of crochet lace. The lace teacher at Cliffoney was Catherine Cosgrove. She came from Lisnaskea, and was trained in the Clones lace factory. Her niece Mrs. Theresa Daly of the Chalet Marietta shop in Cliffoney still continues on the tradition today with a few others, and also teaches the skills and the stitches. At Grange, Margaret Sweeney was the teacher. There is a comprehensive display of the different styles of Cliffoney Lace in the Sligo Museum in Stephen Street.

William Francis Nunan, Ardill's successor, arrived in 1899,(1) and had a long incumbency at Drumcliffe, 33 years. After the grand rededication of the renovated Church it might be thought that the headaches over the maintenance of the church fabric were finally over, but not so, already four years later, in 1899, when a new pulpit in memory of John Wallace was being dedicated at a special service, the offertory collection was in aid of the fund for repairing the church tower.

One of the first events of Nunan's incumbency was that the older portion of the graveyard, that further from the Church building, was transferred to the Rural District Council. The idea of dividing the two halves with a wall was, happily, never put into practice. The arrangement worked fairly well, until in 1925 the Council complained that donkeys were trespassing into the graveyard - so the sexton's wife was asked to keep the gate closed. An intriguing insight into Drumcliffe parish life at this time is the fact that in 1909 it was decided that a cross would be allowed on a gravestone - provided it was a Celtic one!(2) One of the main problems for the Vestry in the early part of the century seems to have been keeping hens and cows out of the graveyard.

WAR, INDEPENDENCE AND CIVIL WAR

The first major crisis in the twentieth century was the Great War of 1914-1918. Ireland was still under British rule and many of her sons, both Unionists and Nationalists, fought and gave their lives in that war, including a number of parishioners from Drumcliffe. In 1919 war memorials were erected on the walls of both Lissadell Church and St. Columba's Drumcliffe and a separate plaque to a parishioner of Lissadell Church, Joseph William Little, who died of wounds on the Island of Lemnos on 17th September 1915.

Lissadell Church was served by the same rector for the First World War and most of the Second World War, the popular bachelor Samuel Miller. Miller was said to have had a lovely friendliness and an ability to talk naturally to people of every age and rank.(3) From those days parishioner George Siggins remembers the stables behind the school housing 10 or 12 horses each Sunday, and several traps. Two families, the Hunters and the Gore-Booths, had carriages, which would be ready and waiting for them at the door of the church at the end of the service. The Hunters, clergy daughters who lived in Raughley, would give Mr. Miller a lift home to the rectory each Sunday; but their attentiveness to him did not extend to listening to his sermons, apparently they read the newspaper, with much rustling, during the sermons!

The Battle Honour Roll at Lissadell includes eleven men and one woman of the parish who served in various different regiments, and the Drumcliffe Memorial lists seven dead and fifteen who served. (Appendix E gives a lists of their names). A new communion table was also given to Drumcliffe Church in memory of the fallen, but for some reason a Mr. Cunningham objected to it. The bishop was called in to deal with this unprecedented situation, and he suggested a slight modification in the design, which seemed to satisfy all parties.(4)

The Easter Rising of 1916 impinged on Sligo with the imprisonment of Constance Markievicz. She was the daughter of Sir Henry Gore-Booth. She married Polish count Casimir Markievicz, who had been a fellow art student with her in Paris. Her sister was Eva Gore-Booth, the poetess, suffrage worker and social worker, best known for her poem "The Little Waves of Breffni". Their father Sir Henry Gore-Booth made several expeditions to the Arctic circle taking his butler Kilgallon with him.

The poet William Butler Yeats had been a visitor to the house for a few days in 1894 and he introduced the younger members of the family to Irish folklore. An unpublished article by former Lissadell guide David Johnston, drawing on a manuscript by Kilgallon, Sir Henry's Butler and companion on his polar expeditions, points out that Yeats probably did not sleep in the house. Kilgallon explained that as they were short of rooms in the main house, they accommodated bachelors in the apartments over the stables, which were equally if not more comfortable. This would make the story that he was awoken by a ghost and met his host Sir Henry on the landing an unlikely one. We know the exact date of one of his visits, from Josslyn Gore-Booth's diaries, one entry recording tersely for

Thursday 22nd. November 1894: "The Poetical Man left". A swamp in the woods opposite one of the Lissadell gateways is all that now remains of an artificial lake created so that Constance, who loved sailing but was frightened of the sea, could sail without fear.

The vicar of Lissadell, the Revd Fletcher Sheridan Le Fanu (nephew of the novelist J.S.Le Fanu) invited Yeats back for a return visit to give a lecture on fairy lore in the Lissadell schoolhouse to what Yeats described afterwards in a letter to his sister Lily as an audience of orangemen.(5) Yeats appears to have had some influence over the sisters, as they began to take an interest in things Irish from then on, and he encouraged Eva in her poetry.

Rosses Point too has associations with the Irish Literary Revival. The writer AE (George Russell) stayed there on several occasions. The author Susan Mitchell - a co-worker with Sir Horace Plunkett in the Irish Co-operative Movement and a poet of the Irish Literary Revival - was very fond of the place and wrote several poems about it, notably "The Greenlands", published in 1904. The Rosses Point road was built by her uncle Noblett St. Leger, who was county surveyor.

CONSTANCE MARKIEVICZ AND EVA GORE-BOOTH

In 1909, together with Bulmer Hobson, Constance Markievicz founded the Fianna na hEireann - a type of Nationalist boy scout movement, which proved a good training-ground for future Irish soldiers. She later joined the Irish citizen army. During the Easter Rising of 1916 she was second in command to Michael Mallin of a battalion which occupied the area of St. Stephen's Green, including the College of Surgeons, on Easter Monday. The following May she was courtmartialled and found guilty of taking part in an armed rebellion and was sentenced to be shot; she was recommended to mercy solely on the grounds of her sex. She was instead given a life-sentence and taken to Aylesbury Prison in England.

In 1918, which was during her time in Holloway Prison, Constance was elected to the House of Commons at Westminster, to represent the St. Patrick's Ward in Dublin, the first woman ever to be so elected. She was however unable to take up her seat. Eva's friend Esther Roper said wistfully "The only sign of Constance there ever was in the British House of Commons was a peg for coats with her name inscribed below" ; this Miss Roper says in her biographical sketch of Constance in the volume she edited of "Prison Letters of Countess Markievicz", in which she also tells of the very close telepathic link between the two sisters.(6) A week after her return to Ireland she was received into the Roman Catholic church at Clonliffe College. After several more sojourns in prison she went on to become Minister for Labour in the first Dail and to work tirelessly for the poor of Dublin.

Eva moved to Manchester and actively worked for the rights of women, especially barmaids, and for pacifism and in the suffragette movement. She did not enjoy good health, but nevertheless managed to publish 12 books, including 10 volumes of poetry and drama before her death in 1926 at the age of 56.

Yeats wrote his famous poem "In Memory of Eva Gore-Booth and Con Markiewicz" in 1927, a year after Eva's death and a few months after Con's. In his Memoirs Yeats tells of his special closeness to Eva, who listened sympathetically as he poured out his sadness over Maud Gonne, and whom he encouraged in her writing, acknowledging that she had real talent.

CO-OPERATIVE SOCIETIES AND OTHER ENTERPRISES

Sir Josslyn Gore-Booth, Constance and Eva's brother, was an active supporter of Sir Horace Plunkett's Agricultural Co-operative Movement, and founded the Drumcliffe Co-operative Creamery in 1895 - the first in the county - and creameries in Ballintrillick and in Ballinfull in 1897. Drumcliffe Creamery produced *Round Tower* brand butter. The creamery is still going today, but it stopped producing butter in the early 70's. In 1904 Cliffoney had its first Agricultural Credit Society, Grange had one in 1914. A Drumcliffe Milling Society followed in 1914, producing *'Benbulben'* brand Oatmeal. The mill was no longer a water-mill at this stage but powered with a gas turbine. The Magherow Potato Growers Society started in 1916. From 1933 until 1935 Cliffoney had its own Turf Cutting Society. The last in the line of North Sligo Societies was in 1955, the North West Cattle Breeding Society. (7)

On Lissadell estate Sir Josslyn had a model dairy farm, a smithy, a pheasantry, forestry and timber trade, and a nursery garden where he grew bulbs, alpine plants and ornamental shrubs as well as forestry trees. Botany and horticulture were hobbies of his. There was also an engineering works on the estate, which manufactured shell cases during the First World War. Beyond Magherow towards Ballyconnell a man called John Edward Martin, who had no legs, started up a shoe factory, around 1910, and also a hotel.

Sir Josslyn's mother Lady Georgina Gore-Booth started a School of Needlework on the estate to teach the women embroidery and crochet, and to give them paid employment. A Miss Flanagan came to teach them and she lived in a flat in the stable block. The school was held in the coachyard and the girls would bring the embroidery home to work on. There was a handsome brochure, with sketches of the chemises, petticoats, berthas, knickers, nightdresses, camisoles, smocks, cushion covers, table cloths, collars, cuffs, handkerchiefs, frocks and infant's day and night gowns, all trimmed with Valenciennes lace and decorated with embroidery, crochet amd drawn thread work. Amongst their customers they counted the Princess Royal, Viscountess Morpeth, the Countess of Aberdeen and Lady Gwendolen Guinness. The embroidery school was next to the estate offices; it was burnt in 1941. Miss Flanagan's nephew, the artist T.P.Flanagan, used to spend his summers with her when he was young.

In 1906 Sir Josslyn acquired one of the early cars in Sligo, a green Torrean with gold lines and yellow wheels. He persuaded an English engineer, Albert

Camisoles, for evening wear, trimmed lace and insertion,

from **6/-**

Camisoles, hand-embroidered in fine nainsook, finished beading and ribbon,

from **5/11.**

Camisoles, hand-made, in fine nainsook, trimmed Valenciennes lace or Torchon lace, fine tucks, beading and ribbon and with puff sleeves,

from **6/6.**

ALL OUR WORK IS ENTIRELY DONE BY HAND.

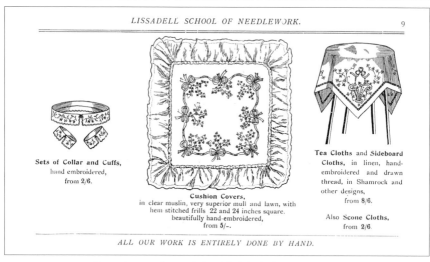

Sets of Collar and Cuffs, hand embroidered, from **2/6.**

Cushion Covers, in clear muslin, very superior mull and lawn, with hem stitched frills 22 and 24 inches square. beautifully hand-embroidered, from **5/-.**

Tea Cloths and Sideboard Cloths, in linen, hand-embroidered and drawn thread, in Shamrock and other designs, from **8/6.**

Also **Scone Cloths,** from **2/6**

ALL OUR WORK IS ENTIRELY DONE BY HAND.

Pages from catalogue of Lissadell School of Needlework

Barnard, who had delivered the car, to stay and teach him how to use it and be his chauffeur. He built Barnard a house near the shore, still known as "the engineer's house". Albert's son Gilbert married Suzanne Hunter, who was the Lissadell schoolmistress for many years. But according to Jim Barber, even more excitement than the car was caused locally by the Lissadell threshing machine.(8)

THE CIVIL WAR

The Civil War between Pro- and Anti-Treatyites, also known as the Free State Army and the Republican Army, was very much felt in Drumcliffe, in spite of the euphemistic title generally given it, of "The Troubles". In 1922 at the base of Benbulben, centring on Ballintrillick on the north and Glencar on the south side of the mountain, six members of the Anti-Treaty forces - known locally as "Sligo's Noble Six" - lost their lives in combat with the Free State Army. Five of them were Sligo men and the sixth a son of Professor Eoin McNeill of Dublin, cofounder with Douglas Hyde in 1893 of the Gaelic League.

Along with many other barracks in the county Drumcliffe Barracks was ransacked and made unfit for habitation, though many other barracks were also burnt. Classiebawn Castle was commandeered and used as a barracks by the Free State Army, and so was Ahamlish Rectory, as was Rahelly. Next four Royal Irish Constabulary police-men were shot dead in an ambush at Moneygold near Cliffoney - this is covered in detail in Joe McGowan's book *In the shadow of Benbulben*.(9) Reprisals included the burning of the Ballintrillick creamery, the Grange Temperance Hall and the Sinn Fein Hall at Cliffoney.

In 1922 the Coast Guard Stations at Raughley and at Rosses Point were burnt. The Eccles family of Moneygold, descendants of the Sodens, had their house raided for arms on three occasions, and Major Eccles was kidnapped at one point along with Sir Josslyn Gore-Booth, Mr. Parkes of Moneygold, Major Myles of Ballyshannon and Mr. Johnson of Kinlough. Ahamlish Church was still open at this time, and the parish was united with Drumcliffe parish. The parishioners of Drumcliffe tried to negotiate a union - or reunion - with Rosses Point as well, but did not succeed in this until the early 1930's, for a short period.

W.B.YEATS

The poet William Butler Yeats and his equally famous brother the painter Jack Yeats spent many summer holidays in Sligo. They stayed sometimes at Avena House Ballysadare, sometimes at Merville in Sligo (now the Nazareth Home) and sometimes at Elsinore at Rosses Point, the Middletons' now ruined

Elsinore at Rosses Point

holiday home by the sea. Rosses Point was beginning to become quite a fashionable seaside resort. But Elsinore had an older history. It was built by a successful smuggler called John Black, who set up several cannon outside it. The house then passed to the Cooper family of Markree, who sold it to William Middleton in 1867. His son Henry Middleton was an eccentric and lived there alone, keeping a herd of Jersey cows and peacocks on the lawn. It was reputed to be haunted by smugglers, who would disclose their presence by three taps on the window-pane.

The brothers would no doubt have visited Drumcliffe where Parson Yeats had lived. The old rectory was still standing then. W.B.Yeats had written in one of his very last poems "Under Benbulben", of his desire to buried there and in it had composed his own gravestone epitaph:

"Cast a cold eye on life on death
horseman pass by." (10)

This epitaph causes much speculation, and people often ask did Yeats ever emerge from his esoteric search for truth and find God? In spite of his early interest in theosophy, while his children were growing up at least he was attending the Church of Ireland Church at Rathfarnham, according to the rector there, who claimed as much in a local or church newspaper. George his wife was eventually buried in the same grave, with a small simple headstone at the foot of the grave.

JACK YEATS

Jack Yeats, William Butler's equally famous brother, both painted and wrote. He had six books published. He started his painting career with watercolours, and at this early stage he painted the attractive "Memory Harbour", featuring Rosses Point, and many of the characters he met locally. His old country characters, whom he and his brother used to know well, reflect his keen observation. There is an excellent collection of these earlier portraits in the Sligo Museum in Stephen Street.

W.B.Yeats Gravestone

He also painted many watercolours of the races on Bowmore Strand, which in early days used to be run on some of the strand as well as the grass between the sandhills. There are a number of earlier oil paintings by Jack Yeats in the remarkable collection in the Niland Gallery above the library in Stephen Street in the converted Congregational Church. Jack Yeats is said to have declared that he never did a painting without a thought of Sligo in it. Certainly he wrote that "Sligo was my school and the sky above it".(11)

SCHOOL PROBLEMS AT LISSADELL CHURCH

In the 1930's one of the Lissadell Vestry's concerns was to keep the number of children attending Lissadell School large enough to justify keeping the school open. Many schemes were tried. The Erasmus Smith School at Munninane had closed by now, and in 1930 bicycles were provided for the Gregg children coming from Munninane to Lissadell School. Then in 1931 a pony and trap were purchased to bring the Lindsay children of Rahelly to school. A debt was incurred over the pony and trap, however, as it was a second-hand one and in bad need of repair and so they had to have a new one made.

The Reverend Samuel Miller, the rector of Lissadell, suggested getting four children from Enniskillen to boost the numbers, but this suggestion was not taken up. The numbers continued to fall badly, and in spite of all the bother about the pony and trap, Mr. Lindsay was very slack about sending his children to school. By 1939 the vestry were declaring that they would continue to lend Thomas Lindsay the pony and trap only so long as he sent the children to the school in it. By January 1940, they demanded the pony and trap back to sell to someone else. They ended up selling it to Lindsay himself for ten pounds - but the ten pounds was payable back to Lindsay to reimburse him for insurance premiums he had paid on the vehicle!

But that was not the end of the saga. In 1945 they again needed a pony and trap to take children to school, and ended up paying for it twice the amount they had received for selling the last one! An added problem was that the Munninane parents objected to children having to travel so far in the winter. Eventually the problem was solved by Louisa Marion Siggins, the schoolteacher at Milltown, who was the sister of Suzanne Barnard the Lissadell schoolteacher. Louisa Marion kindly released some of her pupils from Milltown, to go to Lissadell school instead. Life was fairly problem-free on Lissadell Vestry after that, except that in 1951 when they requested the sexton to keep the church door open, she promptly resigned!(12)

THE WILSONS

After Canon Nunan's departure in 1932, the Reverend John Allen became Rector of Drumcliffe, for a period of five years, until his death.(13) He is buried in the churchyard. During Allen's incumbency, Rosses Point had ceased to be a separate parish, and returned to be with Drumcliffe once again. His five years seem to have been uneventful ones.

The Reverend James Wilson, later Dean Wilson, and his family moved into the Rectory in 1937. They were the last rector and family to live in the old Rectory. They stayed twenty-five years and they were on the whole happy times. Two tragedies occurred during their lives at Drumcliffe. One was the death of double pneumonia at his boarding school in England of their only son and eldest child, Noel Fosbrooke Wilson, at the age of fifteen. The other of course was the Second World War. In 1939 shortly before the outbreak of war there was local excitement when eight separate fires were seen on the island of Inishmurray, from the mainland. Local boats went out and found the inhabitants were desperately short of food owing to stormy weather, and had been signalling for help using a time-honoured method. Help was duly given. Then in 1947 more excitement in the same district as a dead whale was washed up on Ardtrasna beach. Its remains are on display at the Natural History Museum in Merrion Street, Dublin.

Drumcliffe Rectory Courtyard

The canon worked hard growing flowers as well as vegetables, and he kept seven beehives in the walled garden. The courtyard, which is still standing today, was in full use, with their three milking cows, hens, ducks and chickens, and another shed for the car. The Wilsons employed maids, a housekeeper, a gardener and a farm hand. Mrs. Wilson played a full part in the parish too, playing the organ, training the choir, and teaching in Sunday School. Canon Wilson arranged the re-interment of Yeats in 1949. His daughters Doris and Daphne remember a happy childhood at Drumcliffe and maintain that the rectory was haunted by a white monk who entered through a former door in the old bathroom.(14) During Dean Wilson's time the Yeats Summer School was founded, in 1959. See the section on this further on.

THE EMERGENCY
The Second World War was also known as "The Emergency" as Ireland remained neutral. However this neutrality was a rather diluted neutrality.(15) De Valera had agreed to allow a 'corridor' over the Leitrim and Donegal coast near

Ballyshannon and Bundoran so that American planes could reach the bases at Killadeas and Castle Archdale, near Enniskillen. Dublin was blacked out, and was bombed on one occasion. Food was rationed. A Catalina flying boat landed on Lough Gill, and its crew were given hospitality at Haslewood. A great number of Irishmen fought in the war as private individuals rather than in any official national capacity.

A local defence was organised and two men at a time would man a lookout overlooking the sea at Mullaghmore and Knocklane in case a plane lost its way or dropped a bomb. Three or four aeroplanes did crash here during the war years. In 1942 a *B 17* bomber crashed at Bunduff strand at Mullaghmore, but all five of the crew survived. In December 1943 another *B17* landed on top of Eagle Rock near Truskmore, two men were killed and ten survived. A *Martinet* crashed in the sea off Mullaghmore, and in 1945 a Halifax came down in Mullaghmore with two dead and six survivors. The planes were all from America and part of the planning for the Normandy invasion; the B17 was a huge and very heavy bomber, nick-named *The Flying Fortress.* They would fly over the Atlantic straight to Enniskillen to refuel before proceeding to England.

One of the first people to the spot after the Truskmore crash was Dr. Connolly a woman doctor from Cliffoney, who gave medical attention to the ten survivors, and spent most of the night ministering to them, and later insisted on not being paid any expenses. Mrs. Rooney of Cliffoney made tea for the crew and the stretcherbearers. Carl Jones-Henry of Ardtermon also went up to help. He was a Captain in the Local Defence Force, and lived at Ardtermon House near Raughley.

Among those who served with the Allies were the three younger sons of Sir Josslyn Gore-Booth: Hugh, Brian and Angus. Hugh had been a lecturer in estate management at Oxford University, and a land agent in England; at the outbreak of war he joined the Royal Irish Fusiliers and saw action in the Mediterranean as a lieutenant. In November 1943 he fell in action on the island of Leros in the Aegean, aged 33. At first he was reported missing, and the news of his death was only confirmed in March 1944. His father died five days later.

Brian had joined the Royal Navy Volunteer Reserve before the war, having been educated at Dartmouth. He had set up his own literary agency in London, but was called up as a sub-lieutenant at the outbreak of hostilities. He was killed, aged 27, when his ship H.M.S. Exmouth was torpedoed on 21 January 1940, with all hands lost.

Although he served as a captain in the Irish Guards, Angus survived the war and outlived all his brothers and sisters. He died at Lissadell in 1996, aged 75.

In 1949 their mother presented Lissadell Church with two beautiful stained glass windows in memory of Brian and Hugh, "Courage" and "Love", by stained-glass artist Kitty O'Brien, of the well-known Dublin studio *An Tur Gloine*(Tower of Glass).

The two sisters who stayed at home - Gabrielle and Aideen - were extremely plucky. Gabrielle played the organ in Lissadell Church for many years - energetically worked by hand by the sexton Mrs. Lindsay - as well as running Classiebawn estate for Lord Mountbatten. She died of cancer in 1973 and the organ she played has been restored in her memory and fitted with an electric pump in place of the handle. Aideen won a third prize in her debut at the Dublin horseshow aged 74. Both sisters rode side-saddle. She took a great interest in all local affairs and people and conducted tours herself for many years when the house was opened to the public, with great panache. She died in 1994.

DEATH OF W.B.YEATS

W.B.Yeats died in 1939, aged 73, in Roquebrune near Cap Martin in the Alpes Maritimes, where he had gone for health reasons. He said to his wife George a week before his death, that if he were to die there he should be buried there on the hillside and after a year or so dug up and brought to Sligo. A special meeting was called of Drumcliffe parishioners to pass a vote of sympathy to the widow of W.B.Yeats, and to offer a site for the last resting place of the great Irish poet. But as the war intervened, it was nine years before, thanks to the exertions of Sean MacBride, the son of Maud Gonne, Minister for External Affairs at the time, Yeats's remains were brought back to Drumcliffe, the burial place of his choice. This was not done quietly and privately - he was returned to his own country with all pomp and ceremony, as befitted a great poet.

It was in fact an occasion of real celebration. The Dean of St. Patrick's had also offered burial in the Cathedral, which was a great honour, but rather than accepting this, the poet's expressed wishes were carried out. The coffin was carried home in September 1948 in an Irish corvette the Macha, docking at Galway, and on reaching Sligo was piped and drummed to Drumcliffe. His wife George, son Michael and daughter Anne were there to welcome his remains.

Parishioner Bertie Monds, who dug the grave and had it beautifully lined with moss and flowers, and who features incidentally in the foreground of the photograph, was awaiting the arrival of the funeral procession, when he had an urgent message to enlarge the grave by two feet; then soon afterwards another to enlarge it by a further three feet. These efforts turned out to be unnecessary, and Monds attributes this prank to the jealousy of the Galway undertakers that a Sligo firm, Messrs. Lyons, were chosen to provide the hearse!

An interesting photographic record of the funeral is to be seen in the Sligo Museum in Stephen Street. Frank O'Connor, Lennox Robinson, Lord Longford and many other celebrities attended the funeral service. Although the fiftieth anniversary of the reburial went unnoticed by Irish Television, American television did cover it, which gives an idea of how widespread W.B.Yeats's fame has become.(17)

At the suggestion of librarian and art collector Nora Niland, artist Bernard MacDonagh painted a mural on the subject of the Wanderings of Oisin in 1955 as a tribute to W.B.Yeats and Jack Yeats and the Yeats family from the people of Sligo. This has been displayed in the Town Hall until recently, when the building's re-furbishment made the wall on which it was displayed no longer available. Many local people are strongly hoping that this fine painting will be adequately displayed when a large enough venue can be found for it in Sligo or elsewhere.

W.B.Yeats' re-burial at Drumcliffe showing Michael, Anne and George Yeats,
with Bertie Monds the gravedigger in the foreground
-Photo by the late Frank Kerrin. Courtesy of Helen Kerrin

PART IX: MODERN TIMES

THE IRISH REPUBLIC

In 1949 the Irish Republic was established. There were many changes. The large estates such as those belonging to the Mountbatten, Parke, Eccles (descendants of the Sodens) and Gore-Booth families were subdivided among local families, and they no longer employed a large force of servants with dairy-maids, cooks, butler, housemaids, gardeners and handymen etc. This meant that unemployment now became a problem. Only two-thirds of the men of North Sligo were fully employed all year round, as tourism was a seasonal industry. Although the population of Sligo town was increasing, that of the rural area was decreasing, with only one half of the men married.

Agricultural Shows were a great incentive to hard work and high stan-dards. Grange has had an agricultural show since 1945. These country shows include sections for home-baked bread, scones, cakes and jams and embroidery, crochet work and flower arranging as well as livestock, crops and vegetables. Recent competitions have included tractor-reversing, rolling the bale, the best dressed lady and the bonniest baby. In the 1960's a Feis or music festival was started in Carney, with traditional music, verse speaking and Irish dancing competitions.

For the women not only were there branches of the Irish Countrywomen's Association in Magherow, Carney and Cliffoney, but a ladies' football team was started in 1976 representing Drumcliffe and Magherow. Grange has grown in importance and now has the most industry of any North Sligo village, with Sligo Crystal, Lissadell Meats and several joinery and furniture factories and a tile centre. Although Lang's pub, the oldest pub in the village of Grange, has modernised its lounge, the shop and public bar remain delightfully as they were, complete with snug. A small park has been built in the village called St. Molaise's park, with an extremely good fibreglass replica of the oaken statue of St. Molaise, and a semi-circle of standing stones (called locally 'the wishing stones' - appar-ently you have to walk away from them backwards). In 1987 a Sports Centre was built at Oxfield, in former years a home of a branch of the Gore family.

Other new enterprises in the parish at the time of writing are a pottery at Rathcormack, clay sculptures of fairies made at Ardtermon, a cattery and kennels at Lislary, lobster fishing at Cloonagh and Raughley (where the pier was recon-structed by the Sligo County Council in 1980, accommodating 11 fishing boats), self-catering cottages at Ardtermon, oyster and clam farming at Lissadell, an I.S.P.C.A. dog shelter at Cullaghbeg, and the Chalet Marietta at Cliffoney, selling local antique and modern crochet-lace. There are also classical music recitals at Drumcliffe Church, the La Sagesse School for the Mentally Handicapped, a Pitch and Putt course and golf driving range at Lisnalurg, an Alzheimers Disease Day-Care Centre in the converted and renovated Rosary National School at Dunally, and numerous restaurants, hotels and guesthouses.

THE YEATS SUMMER SCHOOL

In 1959 the Yeats Summer School was founded. It was the brain-child of Frank Wynne, Sheelah Kirby and Dr. Tom Henn, Master of St. Catherine's College Cambridge. Thomas Rice Henn was Irish, of the family the Henns of Paradise in Co. Clare. His father was a Rural Magistrate in Sligo, and his sister was married to one of the O'Hara family of Annaghmore near Collooney. Dr. Henn was the longest-serving President of the Summer School.

The Swan Doors at Drumcliffe Church

The School has been a great success, attracting Yeats scholars and students from all over the world. The beautiful swan doorhandles on the West door of the church are the gift of the Yeats Society of Perth in Australia. The school has given the impetus to the founding of the Hawk's Well Theatre and the performing of Yeats plays on an annual basis. The Inaugural Service has traditionally been held at St. Columba's Church Drumcliffe, the addresses over the years being given by a variety of distinguished speakers.

For many years the occasions of the Inauguration were enhanced by the singing of a choir gathered together for the occasion by Louisa Marion Siggins - known as Louie. This remarkable and energetic woman after her retirement kept the church choir going for many years, only retiring at the age of 94 at her family's insistence. She had been parish schoolteacher, parish secretary, church organist, choirmistress and social organiser, and since her death in January 2000 she has been greatly missed.

The Siggins Family's Thaatched Cottage in Cashelgarron

THE REVEREND DEREK HAMILTON

In 1963 Mr. Hamilton arrived and took up residence in the new modern rectory built in the orchard of the old rectory.(1) The old rectory had been sold the previous year to Commandant Vinnie Bligh, who eventually demolished it in 1977 as it was unsafe, and built a large elegant modern house on the site. During Mr. Hamilton's incumbency a special Yeats centenary service took place at St. Columba's church Drumcliffe, which was broadcast on Radio Eireann.

Modern Drumcliffe Rectory

This new rectory could well be the fifth post-reformation Rectory. The first was the one called *Minevoriske*, known about in Elizabethan times,(2)described as being on the river 'between two bridges', which we could interpret as being between Sligo bridge and Drumcliffe bridge which would give us little idea of its location, or as being between Drumcliffe and Collinsford bridges, which would be more helpful if we were sure that there was a Collinsford bridge at that period. The second was the one described as a house belonging to the parson of Drumcliffe at the western end of the church(3). The third was *Seaview*, in Cregg, where Mickey Yeats later lived.(4) The fourth was the big old late eighteenth century rectory, the predecessor of the present one, possibly built in the time of the Reverend Richard Wynne. This dating is a conjecture based on the fact that the rectory was impropriate to his brother Owen, who then owned the tithes and had the patronage of it and could choose the vicars. It also is based on the system which was in operation at the time. In those times there often was no rectory as the previous one was in ruins. The rule in such a case was that the rector then had to build one himself, its value equalling at least one year's stipend. Then his successor when he came was obliged to buy it for 75% of what had been paid for it.

In 1964 the Eccles family of Moneygold offered to pay for the removal of the two old early eighteenth century memorials of the Soden family from the earlier Ahamlish church, which were now on the wall of Ahamlish Church, which was no longer being used. The vestry were not willing to have them inside the church, so Major Eccles suggested the inside of the church porch, to which they agreed and the project was duly carried out.(5) These are worth looking at, as it is rare to see monumental sculpture of this era in such a good state of preservation. In 1967 Milltown School was closed down by the Department of Education.

Memorial to Thomas Soden in Drumcliffe Church Porch, originally from Ahamlish

And in 1968 Ahamlish church was officially closed down. The furniture from it was given to Munninane chapel of ease and the bell was sold to the late D.F.Clarke of Enniskillen, a collector and a friend of the Eccles family.(6) The graveyard is large and is still very much in use by the Roman Catholic community of Cliffoney. The wall was recently rebuilt by F.A.S.

CANON MAURICE SIRR

In November 1969 a new rector, the Reverend Maurice Sirr arrived.(7) The parish had an eventful period during his ministry. His first act was to arrange for the official de-consecration of Ahamlish church. But storm insurance payments were to be kept up for the time being. Captain Stuart of the Church Army conducted a mission near the start of Sirr's ministry in the parish of Drumcliffe with Lissadell and Munninane, and one of the purposes of this was to bring the parishioners closer together; this was a great success. In 1970 the problems of the Vestry were rats and beetles - rats in the graveyard and beetles in the roof timbers.

In March 1975 a special meeting (for everyone, not just the Vestry) was called to discuss the east wall decoration. Church members were asked to decide whether to leave the wall as it was, to repaint it in fresh, different colours, or to paint the wall grey or white and hang a large wooden cross on it. The majority voted to leave it as it was. Later that same year the parishioners voted against amalgamating with Calry Parish. In 1977 a woman churchwarden was elected for the first time in Drumcliffe, Mrs. Elizabeth Barber. She was a great success and more women churchwardens followed. Rosses Point had their first a few years later, Mrs. Shirley Dunne.

In August 1979 a great tragedy happened in the parish, the assassination of Lord Mountbatten with some of his family, off Mullaghmore. (See the separate section on this below).

In 1982 great agricultural improvements were instituted in the district under the tutelage of ACOT, a government programme.(8) The use of silage now became widespread, and overwintering of cattle indoors, and giving ewes supplementary feeds, and other similar improvements.

In 1984 the Lissadell Youth Centre was officially opened by Dail Representative Ted Nealon. The idea for this project was sparked off ten years earlier when a Dublin troop of cub scouts requested the use of the Lissadell school for their summer camp. This was agreed to, and five years later the idea of converting the old school - now unused - into a youth and conference centre was put forward. The parishioners worked hard to raise the money for this. In Youth Year - 1986 - the girl guides planted a copper beech tree in the grounds of the school.

In 1985 the old stables were converted into a shop and coffeehouse, to cater for the large numbers of tourists who came all through the summer months to see Yeats's grave (See the section on this below). In 1987 lightning struck the church tower, doing £5,000 of damage; and also causing a hole in Yeats's grave.(9)

LORD MOUNTBATTEN

How Earl Mountbatten of Burma came to own Classiebawn Castle at Mullaghmore is somewhat complicated. Mountbatten's wife Edwina Countess Mountbatten inherited the castle as she was the granddaughter of the heir of the Hon. Evelyn Ashley, who had inherited it from his uncle William Francis Cooper, Lord Mountemple. Ashley was the son of Lord Shaftesbury the great Victorian philanthropist. Lord Mount Temple had inherited it from his stepfather, the Third Viscount Palmerston, one of Queen Victoria's Prime Ministers. In Palmerston's day the estate consisted of more than 6,000 acres. Palmerston's immediate family, the Temples were granted the land in the mid-seventeenth century.

Lord Mount Temple completed the building of the castle left unfinished by Palmerston, who had stayed at the Cliffoney Hotel during the building of the castle.(10) Little of this eighteenth century inn now remains, and the Mullaghmore public lavatories have been built on the spot where the lime kiln for making the lime mortar for building of the harbour was situated. The castle was built in yellow-brown sandstone shipped by sea from Donegal, and the architect was J. Rawson Carroll. The castle has one central tower with a conical roofed turret, in Scottish baronial style; otherwise it is a normal gabled house. During the first two decades of the second half of the twentieth century, Lord Louis Mountbatten was a familiar figure at Mullaghmore during the month of August, and often seen shrimping under the harbour bridge.

Earl Mountbatten of Burma sold the castle to Hugh Tunney in 1976, with an agreement that the castle, and *Shadow V* his boat, would be available to the family in the month of August each year. On Monday 27th. August 1979 fifty pounds of explosives blew up the boat with a large party of the family aboard, just round the head at Bishop's Point. Lord Louis (as he was known locally) died instantly; his daughter Patricia's mother-in-law the eighty-two year old dowager Lady Brabourne died in hospital the next day; Nicholas Knatchbull, Lord Louis's grandson was killed; and also Paul Maxwell from Enniskillen.(11)

As well as these appalling deaths, three members of the family were seriously injured - Lord Mountbatten's daughter Lady Patricia Brabourne, her husband Lord Brabourne, and their son Timothy Knatchbull, the fifteen-year-old twin brother of Nicholas. As an example of the shock and sorrow felt by people in Sligo over the tragic episode I will quote in full the letter of sympathy sent by the Drumcliffe Vestry to Lady Pamela Hicks, Lord Mountbatten's other daughter.

LETTER OF SYMPATHY
29th. August, 1979. To Lady Pamela Hicks.

We, the Select Vestry of Drumcliffe Parish, of which Mullaghmore is a part, wish to express our deepest sympathy on the tragic loss of life and serious injury which happened at Mullaghmore on the 27th. August. We shared the general feeling of pride in the fact that Lord Mountbatten with his family came each year to holiday at Classiebawn despite the serious political situation in the North of Ireland.

We feel shocked and ashamed that a crime such as this could have occurred. We pray that the comfort of God may be with all who have been bereaved, and that those now injured will soon be restored to full health.

Signed: J. Maurice G. Sirr, Rector; and Louie M. Siggins, Secretary of Drumcliffe Select Vestry.(12)

THE STABLES

A new building project undertaken very successfully during the incumbency of the Revd Maurice Sirr was the conversion of the old stables into a coffee shop and gift shop. The architect was Kevin Kaufman, and The Stables Gift and Coffee Shop was opened in 1985. This facility has enhanced the area as a visiting place for tourists, and also a large car and coach park has been constructed.

The archaeological dig which preceded this work produced much of interest. Archaeologist Joyce Enright in her report explains that the remains discovered indicate that the monastic settlement and its surrounding village had a thriving economy, and were manufacturing iron, pottery, bronze, glass, and bone and antler crafts. She lists exciting finds such as kilns, furnaces, hearths, storage-pits, knives, buckles, nails, decorative jewellery and clay pipes. She also found remnants of the settlement's diet, such as cereal seeds, nuts, bones of sheep, pigs, cows, horses, deer, goats, wildfowl, fish and oysters - the sort of details that make their lives become even more vividly real to us.(13)

CANON ROBERT HAYMAN

Canon Hayman came to Drumcliffe in March 1988, straight from San Francisco, where he had served as rector of St. Luke's, having previously served as archdeacon of Olympia. It is one of the strengths of the Anglican Communion that an Anglican (or as the name is in America, an Episcopalian) from any part of the world can transfer perfectly smoothly to another parish in a different English-speaking country.

During Hayman's incumbency the Youth Centre at Lissadell enjoyed a period of plenty of use. His wife Sally took an interest in this and took over the bookings of the centre; she was also one of the guides at Lissadell House.

During Hayman's incumbency the Armada Memorial at Streedagh was unveiled. This was built in memory of the twelve hundred people who died at Streedagh following the wrecking of the three large ships. The unveiling took place exactly 400 years later, to the day, on 6th. September 1988. A future project planned for the Grange and Streedagh area is an Armada Study Centre. In 1991 there was another tragedy at Mullaghmore, when a diver went missing, a local father of four children. Every available boat joined in the search for him, and Mullaghmore hummed with activity and anxiety as even helicopters came and joined the search. He was eventually found, but it was too late to save his life.

The Haymans stayed in the parish for four years, and have now returned to the United States of America, living in Seattle, nearer their son and daughter.

CANON IAN GALLAGHER

Canon Ian Gallagher is from a Derry family, and was formerly a choirboy in St. Columb's Cathedral, Derry. He worked in the business world before training for ordination and came to the parish in 1993 straight from his curacy in Belturbet and Cootehill Co. Cavan. He has worked tirelessly on several different projects during his time so far. First he organised a project in 1996 to renovate St. Kevin's chapel of ease at Munninane. This has been very tastefully done, using F.A.S. labour. The money for the scheme was raised by an 'Auction of Dreams and Promises' at the local pub, Cissie Mac's at Cashelgarron. This is an auction where the items being auctioned are not present in the building.

His next project was to arrange for the consecration of a new section of the land around Lissadell Church as a graveyard, in addition to the Gore-Booth plot. The first people to be buried there were Holger Schiller of Ardtermon and his son-in-law Fionn Murray, who both died tragically in a planecrash.

Canon Gallagher's largest project so far has been the new visitor centre at Drumcliffe Church. He managed to get funding not only for this but also for much needed repairs to the church, from the International Fund for Ireland and Interreg. The grants were generous, which was fortunate, as once the work on the church was started it became obvious that the church roof was also badly in need of repair. However a large sum of money is still outstanding.

The church roof has been replaced. The walls have been stripped of plaster both inside and on the exterior. The decorated text on the east wall has been repainted by Sligo art students. The stables have been enlarged to twice their original size, which also solved the perennial problem of the need for a church hall. (A small building had been erected at Milltown to serve as a church hall, but it was inadequate and too far from the church and had been let to a carpenter).

During all this building work, great excitement was created by two separate discoveries. The first being the uncovering of the plasterwork to reveal two large portions of a possible decorated high cross, embedded in the wall of the porch and the back wall of the church. The second being the accidental finding of two skeletons during the excavations for the extension to the stables. One of the graves had a stone-washed quartz pebble placed on top, which would date it as in the Mediaeval period - or even very late Mediaeval, as such grave customs tended to continue on for longer in the west of Ireland.(14)

A fifteen minute audio-visual presentation is now shown every half-hour. When it is over the screen silently glides back into its concealed place behind the dado on the east wall. This gives details of St. Columba's life, the Battle of the Books and the founding of the Columban monastery. It places the emphasis once more on St. Columba as the founder of Drumcliffe, while still honouring Yeats as well. The visitor centre was opened by the Taoiseach on St. Columba's Day, 9th. June, 1999. In Autumn 1999 Canon Gallagher's work was acknowledged by his being voted Sligo 'Man of the Year'. In mid-December 1999 lightning hit the tower, but thanks to lightning conductors the damage was not too extensive, with damage to the roof and the south-east pinnacle losing its capstone.

THE NEW MILLENNIUM

Ecumenism is another project of the future which has become a reality already during the incumbency of Canon Ian Gallagher. Ministers of all the main Christian denominations present in Sligo were invited to the opening of the Visitor Centre. Two summers earlier, in 1997, it was the fourteen hundredth anniversary of the death of St. Columba, and it was decided to mark this by a celebration shared between the several Christian churches. There was a shared open air service down by the sea shore near St. Columba's well in Kintogher townland. There was also a special joint Church of Ireland and Roman Catholic service on St. Columba's day begun in St. Columba's Drumcliffe followed by a walk down the half mile road to Rathcormack to St. Columba's Roman Catholic Church for the continuation of the service. During the Week of Prayer for Christian Unity in January 2000 a joint unity service was held in Rathcormack Hall; it is hoped this will be the first of many.

Ideas that have been put forward for future co-operation between the denominations include the exciting one of rebuilding the Round Tower together. Whether or not this will happen we do not yet know. A fund has been started for this project. Certainly the rediscovery of the Celtic strand of Christianity that was practised by St. Columba and his monks, by St. Brigid and her nuns, and Irish Celtic Christians for centuries, is shared between us all. It has so much to offer, with its Christ-centredness, closeness to nature, Biblical basis, warmth of welcome to the stranger, focus on prayer and above all its rich vein of spirituality brought into all of daily life, and expressed through the arts and crafts as well as through all daily work. Rediscovering our common roots in Celtic spirituality has great potential as a uniting factor, as it comes from the time before there were any divisions at all between Catholic, Orthodox and Protestant but all were simply Christians.

Memorial to the late Mary Conway in Drumcliffe Church

APPENDIX A:
Bishops of Elphin and from 1834 Kilmore Elphin and Ardagh, with date of commencement of ministry.

c.435 Assicus
1136 Donal O'Duffy
1152 Maelisa O'Conactain
1181 Thomas O'Connor
1195 Florence McRiagan O'Mulroney
1206 Alan O'Conor
1229 Dionysius O'More
1231 Donatus O'Conor
1245 John O'Hugroin
1246 O'Conor Roe
1247 Thomas O'Connor
1260 Milo O'Connor
1262 Thomas McDermott
1266 Maurice O,Connor
1285 Gelasius O'Connor
1296 Malachi McBrien
1303 Donat O'Flanagan
1308 Charles O'Conor
1310 Malachi McHugh
1312 Laurence O'Laghtnen
1326 John de Roscommon
1356 Gregory O'Meghan
1372 Thomas Barrett
1405 John O'Grada
1412 Thomas Colby
1418 Robert Fosten
1429 Laurence O'Beollayn
1430 Magonius
1444 William O'Hedian
1449 Cornelius O'Melaghlin
1458 Nicholas O'Flannagan
1499 George Brann
1525 John Max
1539 William Maginn

1544 Conal O'Shiel
1552 Roland de Burgo
1580 Thomas Chester
1584 John Lynch
1611 Edward King
1639 Henry Tilson1660 John Parker
1667 John Hudson
1691 Simon Digby
1720 Henry Downes
1724 Theophilus Bolton
1729 Robert Howard
1740 Edward Synge
1762 William Gore
1772 Jemmett Browne
1775 Charles Dodgson
1795 John Law
1810 The Hon. Power Le Poer Trench
1819 John Leslie (last Church of
Ireland Bishop of Elphin alone).
1854 Marcus Gervais Beresford
1862 Hamilton Verschoyle
1870 Charles Leslie (April)
1870 Thomas Carson(September)
1874 John Richard Darley
1884 Samuel Shone
1897 Alfred George Elliott
1915 William Richard Moore
1930 Arthur William Barton
1939 Albert Edward Hughes
1950 Frederick Julian Mitchell
1965 Charles John Tyndall
1959 Edward Moore
1981 Gilbert Wilson
1993 Michael Hugh Gunton Mayes

APPENDIX B:
ABBOTS, ERENACHS ,VICARS AND RECTORS
with date of commencement of Ministry, or dates of death

(a) ABBOTS:
Mothorian 574
Maelpadraig -921
Maengal -930
Murroh O'Bollan -1177
Malachy O'Beollain -1252
Maelfinnan O'Beollain -1254
Maelissa O'Coinel -1330
    O'Beollain - 1362
Maurice O'Coineoil -1416
    O'Beollain - 1503

(b) ERENACHS:
Flann O'Becain - 950
Aengus O'hOenghusa -1029
Murchadh O'Beollain - 1053
Amlave O'Beollain - 1225

(c) VICARS ANDS RECTORS:
(i) Drumcliffe:
Pre-1402 John O'Connel
1403 Dermit Magherleginn
1403 Cornelius O'Coneil
Pre-1414 Cornelius O'Coneil
1414 Charles O'Gara
1425 Dermit O'Coneil
1425 Nemeas O'Beollayn
Pre-1428 Thomas O'Tarpa
1428 Dermit Magaedagan
1446 William O'Beollan
1455 Eugene O'Coneil
1583 Owen O'Conogher
1611 Thomas Pilley
1615 Hugo Hohy
1619 William Rycroft
1661 Robert Browne
1674 James Read
1723 Eubule Ormsby
1730 Edward Munns
1756 Richard Dogherty
1760 Robert Curtis
1767 Michaerl Obins
1783 Thomas Cowper

1785 Stephen Radcliffe
1797 Richard Wynne
1811 John Yeats
1847 Thomas Crawford
1870 Julius Henry Griffith
1877 John Guthrie
1879 James Alan French
1889 John Roche Ardill
1899 William Francis Nunan
1932 John Allen
1937 James Wilson
1963 Samuel Derek Hamilton
1969 James Maurice Glover Sirr
1987 Robert Hayman
1993 Ian Gallagher

(ii)Ahamlish:
1615 Charles O'Connor...   1779 George Hickes...
1886 John Harpur
1635 William Newport...   1770 William Wade...
McCormick
1640 William Young...   1773 Andrew Nixon...
(Then in with Drumcliffe)
1641 Robert Browne...   1774 Matthew Browne...
1674 James Reed...   1776 Charles West...
1723 Eubule Ormsby...   1841 John Evelyn Green...
1766 Andrew Knox...   1881 James Todd...

(iii)Lissadell:
1842 William Jeffcott
1859 Capel Wolseley
1876 Thomas Cosgrave
1885 Frederick Sheridan Le Fanu
1900 William Dudley Saul Fletcher
(later Rector of St. John's Sandymount in Dublin).
1907 Thomas Arnold Harvey
(later Dean of St. Patrick's and then Bishop of Cashel).
1912 Samuel Richard Miller
1943 Cecil Herbert Smyth
1946 Dermot Nichols Bowers
1950 Arthur Cotter

APPENDIX C: CURATES

(i) Drumcliffe:

c. 1764 Andrew Knox....
c. 1775 Anthony Obins...
c. 1783 Hugh Johnston...
c. 1802 John Yeats...
1804 Edward Bullingbroke Ayres
1823 Charles Dunne
1827 George Vaughan Hart...
1832 Edward Lloyd Elwood
1842 Francis Hassard....
1865 John Langford Finnerty...

(ii) Ahamlish:

1730 Edward Munns
1877 John Magill
1881 James Todd

1867 Robert Edward Briscoe.

(iii) Lissadell:

1881 Frederick William Austin

APPENDIX D: CHURCHWARDENS
(A=Ahamlish, D=Drumcliffe, L =Lissadell, M=Munninane, R.P.= Rosses Point)

Alger, James. D. 1844, 1850.
Allen, Charles. D. 1841.
Allen, Matthew, of Rathcormack. D. 1857, 1871-1872.
Anderson, John, of Lislahell;y. D. 1866.
Anderson, James. D. 1807.
Ardill, Kathleen. R.P.1965.
Armstrong, Archibald. D. 1906.
Armstrong, J. of Kiltycooley. D. 1908.
Armstrong, John G. D. 1917.
Armstrong, J. R.P. 1949.
Armstrong, T. R.P. 1955.
Barber, Cecil. D. 1925.
Barber, Elizabeth. D. 1977, 1999.
Barber, Francis. D. 1897.
Barber, Gordon. D. 1991-1993.
Barber, Harold. D. 1997.
Barber, Jack. D. 1953, 1956, 1964, 1973-1974.
Barber, James. D. 1811.
Barber, Jim. D. 1957, 1965, 1972.
Barber, John. D. 1772-1773, 1790-1792, 1867, 1915, 1918.
Barber, John. M. 1988.
Barber, John Lipsett. D. 1904, 1907.
Barber, Joe. D. 1963, 1972, 1985.
Barber, Joe. M. 1991-1993.
Barber Joseph. D. 1876, 1888, 1895, 1902, 1908, 1916.
Barber, Joseph. M. 1974-1981.
Barber, Robert. D. 1982.
Barber, Thomas. D. 1800, 1922, 1936, 1940, 1944, 1947, 1951.
Barber, Tom. D. 1982-1983.
Barber, William, of Ballincar. D. 1794-1797, 1861.
Birne, Philip. D. 1758-1759, 1764-1768.
Bothwell, A. R.P. 1966-1974.
Bourne, Ted. R.P. 1990-1991, 1998-1999.

Boyd, T. M. 1979-1980, 1988.
Bracken, Jules. A. 1955-1956
Browne, R. D. 1915, 1920, 1927, 1932.
Buchanan, Basil. D. 1981.
Buck, Mrs. R.P.,1963-1964.
Burrows, Michael. D. 1914, 1924, 1931, 1938.
Burrows, Robin. D. 1950.
Chambers, Muriel. D. 1979, 1995.
Clark, James. D. 1816, 1846.
Clark, Tallis. D. 1816.
Clarke, B. R.P. 1956.
Clarke, Ben. R.P. 1958,1960-1962.
Clarke, Daniel. D. 1852.
Clarke, Ian. R.P. 1982.
Clarke, Keith. R.P. 1975-1978.
Clarke, Mrs.M. R.P. 1984-1986.
Clarke, Sam. M. 1990, L. 1998.
Clarke, William. R.P. 1949, 1955-1956, 1958, 1960-1974.
Clarke, William, Jr. R.P. 1981, 1988-1991, 1997.
Cooney, Thomas. D. 1910, 1916, 1919, 1923, 1931, 1937.
Craig, J. D. 1925.
Craig, George. D. 1944, 1950.
Cunningham, B. D. 1960.
Cunningham, Charles. D. 1929, 1942.
Cunningham, Jim. D. 1956, 1976.
Cunningham, Patricia. D. 1996.
Cunningham, Samuel. D. 1895.
Dobbs, Frank. D. 1988-1989.
Dodwell, George, of Auburn House, Lisnalurg. D. 1830.
Dorman-Smith, Victor. R.P. 1983-1987. Ian. D. 1989-1990.
Draper, George. R.P. 1977-1979, 1982-1983, 1988-1989, 1996.
Dunne, Ronnie. R.P. 1980, 1987.
Dunne, Shirley. R.P., 1981.
Ewing, T.J. R.P. 1926 - 1931.
East, Henry. D. 1921, R.P. 1932.
Eccles, Major. A. 1926.
Elliott, Sam. D. 1959-1970, 1988.
Ferguson, Matthias, of Cloghbolly. D. 1812-1813.
Ferguson, Robert. L. 1945-1946.
Frizzle, Edward. D. 1875.
Frizzell, John. D. 1886, 1890, 1896, 1903, 1909, 1917.
Frizelle, J. R.P. 1926.
Frizelle, Thomas. R.P. 1927-1931, 1933.
Galbraith, Cunningham. D. 1891.
Giblett, Tony. R.P. 1992-1994, 1998-1999.
Gilmor, J. D. 1959.
Gilmore, William. D. 1889.
Gilmour. D. 1948.
Godsell, David. R.P. 1994-1995.
Greer, S. R.P. 1979.
Greg, James, of Cooladrummman. D. 1866.
Gregg, John, of Barnavalley. D. 1802-1803.
Green, James. D. 1935.

Greene, David. D. 1996.
Greene, L. D. 1971.
Greene, May. D. 1978.
Greene, Noel. D. 1970.
Greene, Robert. D. 1936, 1941.
Griffin, Arnie. D. 1990-1991.
Gore, Sir Booth. D. 1763-1768.
Gore-Booth, Sir Josslyn. L. 1931-1943.
Gore-Booth, Sir Robert, of Lissadell. D. 1806, 1873.
Gore-Jones, John, of Johnsport. D. 1825-1826.
Gowan, John. D. 1784, 1845.
Hamilton, Thomas. D. 1851.
Hamilton, Dr. William, of Urlar House. D. 1849, 1858.
Harrison, James. D. 1757, 1777, 1778.
Harrison, J, D. 1927.
Harrison, Matthias, of Pulmacarron. D. 1787, 1788, 1827.
Harrison, Thomas. D. 1780, 1781.
Henderson, Edward. D. 1890.
Henderson, James. D. 1777, 1778, 1874.
Henderson, John, of Cregg. D. 1807, 1828.
Henderson, John. L. 1991-1993.
Henry, Alby. M. 1965-1971.
Henry, Basil. M. 1982-1987.
Henry, George. M. 1989.
Henry, Pearl. M. 1994-1995.
Henry, Raymond. M. 1981.
Henry, Trevor. M. 1990-1993.
Hood, Freddie. A. 1955, 1956, 1958.
Hudson, John, of Lislahelly. D. 1859.
Hunter, John. D. 1876.
Hunter, J.J. D. 1943.
Hunter, Richard. D. 1980.
Irwin, Richard, of Summerhill. D. 1825,1826.
Irwin, Robert. D. 1814, 1815, 1941, 1942.
Jackson, John, of Tully. D. 1822-1824.
Jones, Christopher. D. 1758, 1759.
Jones, John, of Rockley. D. 1784, 1831.
Jones, Michael. D. 1846, 1847.
Jones, Robert. D. 1761, 1762,1789.
Jones-Henry, C. L. 1979-1980.
Jones-Henry, Charles. L. 1942.
Jones-Henry, Vivian. L. 1968-1970.
Jones-Henry, J.C. L. 1948.
Kerr, John. D. 1854.
Kerr, Robert. D. 1818-1821.
Kerr, Samuel. D. 1848.
Lattimer, E. R.P. 1975-1976.
Lawson, Gordon. L. 1978-1979, 1981-1982, 1984-1995, 1997, 1999.
Lawson, Jack. D. 1975, 1979.
Lawson, Ronald. D. 1985, 1992-1995.
Lawson, Sylvia. L. 1983, 1985-1987, 1994, 1997.
L'Estrange, Capt., of Lisnalurg. C.C.D. 1976-1977, 1981.
Lindsay, Andrew. D. 1874.

Lindsay, John, of Tully. D. 1899, 1905, 1912, 1924.
Lindsay, Robert. D. 1932.
Lumsden, Capt. Alexander, of Cregg House. D. 1854-1856, 1860.
Lyttle, John, of Munninane. D. 1809-1810.
Lyttle, William. D. 1772-1773.
McAdams, William. D. 1884, 1889, 1896, 1902.
McAdams, W.J.Jr. D. 1923, 1928, 1937.
McCadden, William. D. 1877.
McCormack, John. D. 1995.
McGaraghan, James. D. 1911, 1918.
McKim, Philip. D. 1800
McKim, William. D. 1774-1776, 1865.
McLoughrey. William. D. 1850.
Magee, Thomas. D. 1892.
Meldrum, Christopher, of Milltown. D. 1804-1805.
Meldrum, Patt. D. 1798-1799.
Monds, Bertie. D. 1955, 1958.
Monds, Edward. D. 1928.
Monds, H. D. 1926.
Monds, Tom. D. 1954.
Morrison, Matthew A. D. 1868.
Munns, Edward. D. 1789.
Munns, James, of Carnatogher. D. 1802-1803, 1833.
Munns, Thomas, of Carnatogher. D. 1827, 1841.
Munns, William. D. 1774-1776, 1798-1799.
Nairn, Bertie. R.P. 1980.
Nicholson, Edward, of Cregg House. D. 1831.
O'Beirne, William. D. 1760, 1770.
Parke, Edward. A. 1926.
Parke, John. D. 1780-1781, 1843, 1890, 1901, 1907.
Parke, Patrick, of Castlegal. D. 1862.
Parke, Philip, of Castlegal. D. 1845, 1861.
Parke, Capt. Roger. D. 1770-1771.
Parke, Roger, of Dunally. D. 1870-1871.
Parke, Thomas, of Castlegal. D. 1809-1810, 1812-1813.
Parke, Thomas H., of Castlegal. D. 1883.
Parke, William. D. 1791-1793, 1880.
Patterson, Avril. D. 1998.
Patterson, Jim. D. 1962, 1974, 1978.
Patterson, Richard, of Kielty. D. 1933, 1986-1987.
Patterson, Stuart. D. 1994.
Payne, Robert. M. 1986-1987.
Payne. William. M. 1965-1971, 1974-1979.
Payne, Mrs. W. M. 1982.
Payne, W. Jr. M. 1983, 1985.
Reynolds, James. L. 1931-1933, 1943, 1947-1949, 1958, 1965-1967, 1971.
Roe, Dr. D. 1881.
Rogers, Jeremiah. D. 1852, 1855, 1869, 1877.
Rogers, Charles G. of Drumcliffe. D. 1879, 1885.
Schofield, P. R.P. 1933.
Shaw, B. D. 1961.
Shaw, Charles. D. 1934.
Shaw, Florrie. D. 1997.

Shaw, George, of Ballinagollagh. D. 1859.
Shaw, George. D. 1875, 1900.
Shaw, George, of Kilsellagh. D. 1864.
Shaw, George Warren. D. 1832, 1839.
Shaw, Helen. D. 1983.
Shaw, James, of Cooladrummin. D. 1787-1788, 1873, 1885, 1891, 1893, 1897, 1904,
Shaw, James. D. 1873, 1885, 1891, 1893, 1897, 1904, 1910.
Shaw, Johnston. D. 1779, 1793-1796.
Shaw, Joseph. D. 1811.
Shaw, Patrick. D. 1865.
Shaw, Philip. D. 1847.
Shaw, Robert. D. 1782-1783, 1844, 1869, 1874, 1921.
Shaw, Robert, of The Green. D. 1893, 1900, 1906.
Shaw, Robert S. D. 1935, 1940, 1949, 1952.
Shaw, Samuel, of Tully. D. 1785-1786, 1804-1805.
Shaw, Smith, of Ballinagollagh. D. 1842, 1863, 1886.
Shaw, Tom. D. 1929.
Shaw, William, of Ardtrasna. D. 1829.
Shaw. William, of Ballinagollagh. D. 1867.
Shaw, William R.N. D. 1888, 1894, 1901, 1903.
Shaw, W.A. D. 1913, 1926, 1930.
Shaw, W. Wallace. D. 1914, 1922.
Shaw, W. Wallace Jr. D. 1929
Shaw, W. D. 1919.
Shaw, William, of Cooladrummin. D. 1933.
Siberry, James. D. 1938, 1945-1946, 1952, 1958, 1966.
Siggins, C. L. 1944.
Siggins, G. L. 1957.
Siggins, George. L. 1994-1995.
Siggins, J.R. D. 1973.
Siggins, Jennifer. L. 1996.
Siggins, L.R. D. 1975.
Siggins, Reginald. D. 1934, 1939, 1943, 1948-1949, 1951, 1953, 1957.
Siggins, Ronnie. D. 1984.
Siggins, Stanley. L. 1975-1976.
Siggins, Sylvia. 1972-1973.
Siggins, T.R. D. 1969.
Siggins, Trevor. L. 1980-1983, 1986-1993, 1996, 1998.
Siggins, W.F. D. 1898, 1909.
Simpson, Albert, of Rathbraccen. D. 1883.
Simpson, Charles, of Carnatogher. D. 1829, 1851.
Simpson, Charles, of Tully Hill. D. 1863.
Simpson, Edward, of Millbrook. D. 1870.
Simpson, Edward, of Tully. D. 1808, 1856.
Simpson, Thomas, of Carnatogher(or Kinatogher). D. 1862, 1880, 1887, 1891, 1898.
Simpson, William, of Tully Hill. D. 1882.
Smith, A. D. 1913.
Smith. David. R.P. 1992-1993.
Smithwick, William, of Cregg. D. 1868.
Somerville, George, of Urlar. D. 1853, 1864.
Somerville, Montgomery J.P. D. 1887, 1892, 1912, 1920.
Somerville, W. D. 1899, 1905.
Stewart, Thomas. D. 1894.

Thain, Raymond. D. 1984.
Tyler, Richard. D. 1797.
Tyler, Thomas. D. 1757.
Walker, Donald. L. 1961-1972, 1983, 1988, 1999.
Walker, Gordon. L. 1948, 1950-1958.
Walker, Maurice. L. 1959-1961, 1973-1974.
Walker, Victor. L. 1944-1946.
Wallace, George, of Carney. D. 1822-1824, 1832, 1839.
Wallace, James, of Carney. D. 1828.
Wallace, John, of Carney. D. 1857, 1884.
Wallace, Thomas, of Carney. D. 1833, 1848.
Wallace, William, of Carney. D. 1858.
Ward, Desmond. D. 1998-1999.
Ward, Matthias. D. 1760.
Warren, Alexina. D. 1980; M. 1994-1995.
Warren, D. L. 1976.
Warren, David. L. 1989.
Warren, Francis. D. 1779.
Warren, George. D. 1782-1783, 1814.
Warren, George. L. 1949-1956, 1962-1964, 1974-1975.
Warren, John. L. 1934-1941, 1947, 1959-1960, 1977-1978, 1984-1985.
Warren, William. D. 1761, 1762, 1785-1786, 1815.
West, Alan. D. 1986-1987.
West, Arthur. D. 1930, 1946-1947.
West, Desmond. D. 1945, 1955, 1967, 1971.
West, Ian A. D. 1968.
West, Thomas. D. 1911.
Whittaker, William. D. 1891.
Wilson, Charles. R.P. 1932.
Wilson, Robert. D. 1853.
Wilson, William. D. 1842.
Wray, Tom. D. 1954.
Wynne, Col. Owen, of Haslewood. D. 1763, 1806, 1817.
Wynne, Owen. D. 1872.
Wynne, John, of Hazelwood. D. 1830.
Yeats, Thomas, of Bayview, Cregg. D. 1849, 1860.
Young, Alexander, of Attiduff. D. 1808, 1817-1818.
Young, James. D. 1819-1821.
Young, William. D. 1843.

APPENDIX E:

(i)Monuments and Gravestones

There are some attractive and noteworthy monuments from a later age than the high crosses. The old early eighteenth century Soden memorials are in excellent condition, having been kept inside Ahamlish Church; the earlier one is dated 1705. The monuments on the church walls inside, particularly the "Cherub Memorial" to the Parke family, and some of the eighteenth and nineteenth century gravestones are fine monumental sculpture. The box-tomb to Arabella Jones is actually signed which monumental sculpture expert Mary Timoney tells me is very rare. The inscription is elegant with decorative flourishes, and reads "Dun by Manus Flannelly 1801". The skull and crossed bones were typical of the Church of Ireland headstones of this period when crosses and crucifixes were seen to be too 'popish'. The gravestone of Mary Conway is a remarkable carving in slate, a difficult stone to carve. Mary Timoney has discovered that the slate was taken from a quarry on Benbulben and donated by Lord Palmerston. See the photograph of this, showing the two angels' heads on page 118. The slate looks as new as the day it was quarried, and has not aged as the limestone slabs have done. The Revd Michael Obins and his son on their memorial slabs on the east wall have carved cherubs' heads in an attractive and typical design.

Sketch of Flannelly tomb north panel showing skull and crossed bones motif by Stella Durand

(ii) Church of Ireland families that are buried in the parish with gravestones that are decipherable:

DRUMCLIFFE:- Adams, Alexander, Allen (incl The Revd John), Ardill (incl the Revd John Roche), Armstrong, Bailey, Barber, Bolster, Bolton, Browne, Buchanan, Butler, Carter, Chambers, Comrie, Cooney, Craig, Crawford (incl. Revd T.),Cregg, Cunningham, Fairleigh, Faussett, Ferguson, Flood, Frizell, Galbraith, Gillies, Gilmour, Gore, Greer, Gregg, Hamilton, Harrison, Hassard, Hetherington, Hood, Hudson, Hunt, Hunter, Irwin, James, Jeffcott, Jones, Jones-Henry, Kerr, Lewis, Likely, Lindsay, Livesey, McAdams, McCormack, McCullagh, McGuffney, Mackie, Magee, Middleton, Millar, Mitchell, Moffat,

Monds, Mullin, Murray, Nash, O'Beirne, Obins, Oldfield, Ormsby-Jones, Parke, Patterson, Payne, Porter, Porteus, Powell, Roycroft, Roose, Rutherford, Ryan, Shaw, Siberry, Siggins, Simpson, Smith, Smithwick, Soden, Somerville, Stanley, Stevenson, Stewart, Turtle, Walker, Wallace, Waller, Walls, Warren, West, Williamson, Wilson, Young. AHAMLISH:- Allen, Eccles, Elliott, Leeson, Mitchell, Noble, Parke, Pearson, Soden.

(iii) War memorials:-(i) DRUMCLIFFE: J.Cunningham, F.Gillespie, V.Gillespie, V.Kerr, E.G.Monds, W.H.Parke and W.Regan gave their lives in the 1914-1918 War; and G.Barber, J.Barber, J.Browne, E.Cunningham, A.Kerr, W.P.Lindsay, W.McLoughlin, J.McLoughlin, W.K.McMullan, W.A.Nunan, W.Ormsby, R.Shaw, A.West, G.West and W.West fought in the War. (ii) LISSADELL: Albert Barnard, George Bailey, James Moor Baird, Ernest Geroge Berrow, Vyvian Barrett Jones-Henry, Andrew Lindsay, Albert Millar, Henrietta Evangeline Millar, Ephraim Scarff, John Victor Scarff, Frederick Hamilton, Walter Sharpe and James Francis Walker served in the 1914-1918 War, and Joseph William Little gave his life. (This list of names gives us a good idea of how full Lissadell Church must have been in the early part of this century).

(iv)Wall Plaques:(i) DRUMCLIFFE: Allen: Thomasina; Crawford: Adair Francis; Jones: John, Michael, Revd Christopher, John Francis, Michael Obins Seeley; Parke: Sir William, Andrew, Alice Charlotte, Roger, Roger Charles; Johnstone: William; Yeats: John; Wilson: James; Soden: Elizabeth, Thomas. (ii) LISSADELL: Little: William; Jeffcott: William. Catherine Wallis donated the metal Last Supper bas-relief in memory of her parents Edward and Mary Jane Young and her brothers Robert, James and Henry.

ABBREVIATIONS USED

A.C.	Annals of Connaught
A.F.M.	Annals of the Four Masters
A.I.	Annals of Inisfallen
A.L.C.	Annals of Loch Ce
D.V.B.	Drumcliffe Vestry Book (Vol I unless otherwise stated).
G.A.S.J.	Galway Archaeological Society Journal.
I.E.G.	Irish Ecclesiastical Gazette.
I.E.R.	Irish Ecclesiastical Record.
J.R.S.A.I.	Journal of the Royal Society of Antiquaries of Ireland.
L.B.S.L.	James Blennerhassett Leslie's Biographical Succession List - Elphin.
L.H.	Living Heritage.
L.M.B.	Lissadell Minute Book.
L.T.D.	Samuel Lewis: Topographical Dictionary.
M.D.	The Martyrology of Donegal.
O.R.H.S.	O'Rourke's History of Sligo.
P.R.H.A.A.I.	Proceedings of the Royal Historical and Archaeological Association of Ireland.
P.R.I.A.	Proceedings of the Royal Irish Academy.
P.R.O.I.	Public Record Office of Ireland.
P.R.O.N.I.	Public Record Office of Northern Ireland.
R.C.B.L.	Representative Church Body Library.
S.C.L.L.H.C.	Sligo County Library Local History Collection.
S.F.H.R.S.	Sligo Family History Research Society.
W.H.B.	Ware's History of the Bishops.
W.M.H.S.	Wood-Martin's History of Sligo.

NOTES

PART I

1. Quoted in Henry Morris: 'Dun na mBarc and the Lady Ceasair'. *J.R.S.A.I.* 1933, p.71.
2. op.cit. pp.74 - 79, especially p.78.
3. Conversation with Frank O'Connor at Ahamlish House, August 1999.
4. *W.M.H.S.* Vol. I, pp.172/3.
5. *O.R.H.S.* Vol. I, pp. 487/8.
6. Quoted in op. cit. Vol.I, p.491
7. H. O'Neill Hencken : 'A long cairn at Creevykeel'. *J.R.S.A.I.* 1939, pp.53-98.
8. Conversation with Margaret Hedge , owner of land on which Cashelbreen stands.
9. Joe McGowan: *Inishmurray - Gale, Stone and Fire.* 1998. p.15.
10. Richard N. Baily: 'Early Irish Carved Stone'. In *J.R.S.A.I.* Vol.120, 1990. p.128.
11. Colum Kenny: *Molaise.* 1998. pp.101/2.
12. Denis Molaise Meehan O.S.B.: *Molaise of Inishmurray.* 1989. p.19.
13. Coquebert de Mentbert: 'A Frenchman's Tour of Connaught,1791'. In *G.A.S.J.*
14. Henry Morris: *Researches in Local History.* S.C.L.L.H.C. Booklet No. 27, p. 15.
15. Conversation with Dan Gilmartin at Keeloges, August 1999.
16. 'Notes of Home Rambles', anon. art.in *The Irish Monthly*, Nov/Dec 1883, p. 597.
17. W.F.Wakeman: 'On Certain Wells situate in the North West of Ireland; with Remarks on the Occurrence of the Croix Gammee or Swastica, as found at St. Brigid's Well, near Cliffoney Co. Sligo' *J.R.S.A.I.* 1880. pp.18ff.
18. Robert Lloyd Praeger: *The Way that I Went.* 1969. p.145.
19. T. Curtis, R.Goodwillie & R.Young/An Foras Forbatha: *Areas of Scientific Interest in Co. Sligo.* p.76.
20. op. cit. p.52.
21. Dr. Don Cotton: 'Sligo's Undiscovered Wild Places'. *In Living Heritage*, Vol.9, Vol. 1, Spring/Summer 1992. p. 26.
22. Curtis, Goodwillie & Young, op. cit. p.70.
23. Conversation with Frank O'Connor, August 1999.
24. J.P.T.Burchell & J. Reid Moir: *The Early Mousterian Implements of Sligo.* 1928. pp.13-15.
25. Patricia McElhone: *Lift the Latch.* 1994. p.25.
26. *O.R.H.S.* Vol. I, p.481.
27. Loc. cit.
28. Conversation with Brian Haran, Wild Life Officer, August 1999.
29. Dr. Don Cotton loc. cit.
30. Conversation with Dr. Don Cotton, September 1999.
32. Curtis, Goodwillie & Young, loc. cit.
31. *O.R.H.S.* Vol. I, p. 502.
32. Ibid., p. 482.
34. Arthur B. Wynne F.G.S.: *Explanatory Memoir to Accompany Sheets 42 & 43 of the Maps of the Geological Survey of Ireland comprising the Counties of Sligo and Leitrim.* 1885. p.28.
35. Conversation with John Corcoran, August 1999.
36. Conversation with Alfie Butler at Ballinfull, December 1999.
37. Gerry Foley: *A Historical Report on the Gleniff (Barytes) Steam Mill.* 1998. Also personal conversation with Gerry Foley June 1999.

PART II

1. Seaton Milligan: 'County Sligo'. In *J.R.S.A.I.* 1896, pp.310.
2. Henry Morris: *Researches in Local History.* SCLLHC Booklet No. 27.
3. George Otto Simms: *The Psalms in the Time of St. Columba 1963.*
4. *A.U.* 697. Quoted in Daibhi O'Croinin: *Early Mediaeval Ireland 400-1200* 1995. p.80. v. also Gilbert Markus O.P.: *Adomnan's Law of the Innocents,* 1997.

5. *M.D.* p. 165; also in ed. O'Kelleher: *Betha Colmcille*, pp. 88-9.
6. *A.F.M.* Vol. I, p. 571.
7. Joyce Enright: *Introductory Report on the Archaeological Excavation at Drumcliffe Co. Sligo.* 1985. p.5.
8. The Revd W.Henry: *Hints towards a Natural and Topographical History of Sligo.* 1739. p.19.
9. George Petrie: *Journal of a Tour in Sligo,*1837. S.C.L.L.H.C. MS. No.
10. Sheelah Kirby: *A Guide to Drumcliffe.* p.2.
11. ibid. p. 6.
12. The Revd W. Henry:p. 18.
13. *Account Book of Roger Walker of Rathcarrick.* August 1837, p.23. S.C.L.L.H.C. Ms. No. 575.
14. Conversation withe the archaeologist Martin Timoney, July 1999.
15. Aubrey Gwynne & R. Neville Hadcock: *Mediaeval Religious Houses - Ireland.*1970. pp.318/9.
16. ibid. p. 437.
17. *A.F.M.* Quoted in *ORHS* Vol. I, p.506.
18. Conversation with Brian Curran, June 1999.
19. ed. Kathleen Mulchrone: *The Tripartite Life of Patrick.* Vol. I, p.89.
20. *M.D.* quoted in.Revd J.J.Kelly: 'Saint Assicus and the Patron Saints of Elphin'. In *I.E.R* Vol. 14, 1893, p. 291.
21. Samuel Lewis: *A Topographical Dictionary of Ireland.* p.513.

PART III

1. *A.L.C.* Vol. I, p.429.
2. *A.F.M.,* Vol. II, p.667.
3. *A.I.,* p.151.
4. ibid, p.157.
5. *A.L.C.* Vol. I, p.19.
6. M. Sweeney: *Transcript of Lough Gill Cruises Commentary,* 1998. S.CL.H.C. Booklet No. 43.
7. *A.L.C.* Vol.I, p.79.
8. ibid. p.125.
9. ibid. p.133.
10. ibid. p.275.
11. *A.F.M.* Vol. VI. p. 1,983.
12. Walter Harris's Marginal Note in *W.H.B.* 1784, p. 360.
13. *A.F.M.* Vol. III. p. 79.
14. *A.L.C.* Vol. I. p.399.
15. ibid. p. 399.
16. ibid. p. 483.
17. loc. cit.
18. *A.C.* p.211.
19. *A.F.M.* Vol. V, p.1,267.
20. *W.H.B.* p. 633.
21. *L.B.S.L.* pp. 129ff.

PART IV

1. *W.H.B.* p. 633.
2. John Lynch, 1584. Ibid.p. 634.
3. *L.B.S.L.* p. 129.
4. Dominic O'Daly: *History of the Geraldines.* tr. C.P.Meehan 1878.
5. Tony Toher: *Exploring Sligo and North Leitrim.* 1994. p.51.
6. *A Letter written on October 4, 1589, by Capt. Cuellar of the Spanish Armada to his Majesty King Philip II,* tr. Henry Dwight Sedgwick Jr. 1896.
7. Bob Quinn: *Atlantean - Ireland's North African and Maritime Heritage.* 1986. pp.150/1.
8. *L.B.S.L.* p.131.
9. *L.T.D.* p. 513.

10. W.B.Yeats: *Memoirs*, ed. Denis O'Donoghue. 1972. p.78.
11. *A.F.M.* Vol.III, p.179 & *A.F.M.* Vol. IV, p. 753.
12. Henry Morris: 'The Dalys as Irish Bards'. In *The Roscommon Herald,* 17th. March 1928.
13. W.B.Yeats: opening lines of the poem 'In Memory of Eva Gore-Booth and Con Markiewicz' in *The Winding Stair and other poems.* 1933. p. 263 of Collected Poems 1963.
14. Tr. Quiggin, quoted in Henry Morris op. cit.
15. *L.B.S.L.*p.9.
16. Bishop Edward King: *Visitation Report of the Diocese of Elphin,* c.1622. pp. 116-119 of Ms. Z3.1.3, quoted with the permission of the Governors and Guardians of Marsh's Library.
17. *L.B.S.L.* p.131.
18. *W.M.H.S.* Vol. I, Appendix A, pp.141-193.
19. Anne Chambers: *Eleanor Countess of Desmond.* 1986.
20. Op. Cit. p. 226.
21. *L.B.S.L.* p. 131.
22. *Religious Census of the Diocese of Elphin,* 1766.
23. *L.B.S.L.* p.131.
24. The Revd W. Henry, op. cit., pp.19/20.

PART V

1. J. McHale et al: *Eighteenth Century Sligo*, S.C.L.L.H.C. No. 49, p.22.
2. Revd W. Henry, op. cit. p. 17.
3. L.B.S.L. p. 131.
4. loc. cit.
5. Marie-Louise Legg ed.: *The Synge Letters - Bishop Edward Synge to his daughter Alicia, Roscommon to Dublin* , 1746-1752. 1996.
6. Conversation with Martin Waters, August 1999.
7. *W.M.H.S.* Vol. I, p.309.
8. David Dickson: *Arctic Ireland.* 1997.
9. Ibid, pp. 29 & 55.
10. *L.B.S.L.* p.131.
11. Loc. cit.
12. Loc.cit.
13. op. cit. p. 132.
14. Loc.cit.
15. *D.V.B.* p. 83.
16. J. McHale et al *"Eighteenth Century Sligo"*, S.C.L.L.H.C. Booklet No. 49.
17. *L.B.S.L.* P. 132.
18. *D.V.B.* p.144.

PART VI

1. *W.M.H.S.* Vol. III., Appendix B. pp.424/7.
2. John C. McTernan: *In Sligo Long Ago.* 1998. p.113.
3. *W.M.H.S.* Vol. III, pp. 314-321.
4. *D.V.B.* p.109.
5. Alan Acheson: *A History of the Church of Ireland 1691-1996.* 1997. pp.129 & 134.
6 Thomas Cooley: *Book of Drawings.* 1773. Armagh Public Library . Ms. No. Z xxi. 33.
7 Erica Loane: *Architectural Drawings by Thomas Cooley in the Public Library, Armagh.* LB.I:15
8. Ibid p.127.
9. F.E.Wagner: *History and Succession List of the Clergy of Elphin.* p.10.
10. *D.V.B.* p.157.
11. *O.R.H.S.* Vol. II, p.28.
12. Conversation with David Griffin of the Irish Architectural Archive, July 1999.
13. *L.T.D.* p.22.

14. Jan Eccles: *A Twentieth Century Life in Ireland*. 1996. p.20.
15. J.C.Curwen: *Observations on Sligo and Surroundings*. 1818. p. 283.
16. *Adamnan's Life of Columba*, ed. William Reeves. 1874. p. 287.
17. Stanley Lane-Poole: *North-West by North*. 1903. p.26.
18. *D.V.B.* p. 184.
19. *O.R.H.S.* Vol. II, p.27.
20. W.B.Yeats: *Reveries over Childhood and Youth*, 1915, pp. 22 & 21.
21. *Dune Management in the West of Ireland - Co. Sligo*. S.C.L.L.H.Booklet No. 51.
22. *D.V.B.* p. 203.
23. *The Sligo Journal*, June 5th. 1822.
24. *School-masters and School-mistresses in Co. Sligo Ireland*, 1826-7. Arr. Dorothy Rines Dingfelder. S.C.L.L.H.C. T/S No. L.H.37.
25. Patrick Cumin: *Report of the Royal Commission of Enquiry into Primary Education in the North-West*. 1870. Tables on pp. 123ff.
26. Henry Irwin M.D.: *A Record of the Cholera Asiatica as it occurred in Sligo in the months of August & September 1832*. 1832. p.2.
27. *W.M.H.S.* Vol.III, p. 73.
28. Jonathan Binns: *The Miseries and Beauties of Ireland*. 1837. pp. 340-343.
29. Ibid. p. 355.
30. John C. McTernan: *Memory Harbour - The Port of Sligo*. 1992. p.80.
31. Stephen Coote: *W.B.Yeats - A Life*. 1997. p.4.
32. W.B.Yeats: *Autobiographies*. 1955. p.53.
33. Deirdre Ryan: *Sir Robert Gore-Booth - Famine and Emigration, 1845-1847*. U.C.D.MA thesis. Chapter 1, page 1.
34. John C. McTernan: op. cit. p.33.

PART VII

1. Estella Carter: *The Famine of Co. Sligo, 1845-1847*, from Local Newspaper Reports. S.C.L.L.H.C. Ms. No. 72. p.24.
2. *L.B.S.L.* p. 132.
3. F.W.E.Wagner: *History and Succession-list of Clergy of Elphin*. 1864. p.11.
4. *W.M.H.S* Vol. III, p.36.
5. John C. McTernan: *Olde Sligoe*. 1995. pp.396/9..
6. John C. McTernan: *Memory Harbour - The Port of Sligo*. 1992. pp.95-97 & 105.
7. Private letter written to John C. McTernan. In Gore-Booth papers, S.C.L.L.H.C. Ms. No. 535.
8. Conversation with David Griffin of the National Architectural Archive, in August 1999.
9. Nicola Gordon-Bowe, David Caron & Michael Wynne: *Gazetteer of Irish Stained Glass*. 1988. p.73.
10. *I.E.G.* Vol. I, June 1858.
11. Conversation with Jim Barber, July 1999.
12. David Willis: 'New Roles for Old Houses - Country Houses of Sligo'. *In Living Heritage*, Vol. IX. 1992.
13. Conversation with Drummond Nelson, September 1999.
14. *DV.B.* p. 299.
15. Ibid p.292.
16. Ibid. p.293.
17. *O.R.H.S.* Vol. II, p.28.
18. *L.B.S.L.* p. 133.
19. Loc.cit.
20. John C. McTernan: *Olde Sligoe*. 1997. pp. 411-415.
21. 'Notes of Home Rambles'. Anon. art. in *The Irish Monthly*, Nov./Dec.1883. p.598.
22. John C. McTernan: *Worthies of Sligo*. 1996. pp.261-264 & 346-349.
23. *L.B.S.L.* p.133.
24. John Roche Ardill: *Forgotten Facts of History*. 1905. pp.6-8.

25. Ibid. p.35.
26. Loc. Cit.
27. John Roche Ardill: *St. Patrick A.D.180.* 1931.
28. *D.V.B.* p.355.
29. *I.E.G.* October 1895.
30. *Sligo Champion* and *Sligo Independent,* early October 1895.

PART VIII

1. *L.B.S.L.* p. 133.
2. *D.V.B.* p. 379.
3. Conversation with Alfie Butler, December 1999.
4. *D.V.B.* p. 401.
5. Letter to his sister Lily, December 16th. 1894. In *Collected Letters of W.B.Yeats* Vol. I, 1865-1895, ed. John Kelly & Guy Domville. 1986.
6. Esther Roper: Biographical Sketch in Prison *Letters of Countess Markeivicz.*1987. p.88.
7. S.C.L.L.H. Ms. No. 367.
8. Conversation with Jim Barber. July 1999.
9. Joe McGowan: *In the Shadow of Benbulben.* 1993. pp. 113-129.
10. Stanza VI of 'Under Benbulben', in *Last Poems,* 1938. pp.400-401 of Collected Poems, 1963.
11. T.G. Rosenthal: *Yeats.* In 'The Masters' Series, No. 40. p.2.
12. *L.M.B.* pp.98 & 199.
13. *L.B.S.L.* p.133.
14. Conversation with the sisters in July 1999.
15. Bernard McDonagh's felicitous phrase; to whom I am also greatly indebted for the loan of material on the 'plane crashes.
16. Letter to the author from Canon Robert Hayman, December 1998.

PART IX

1. *D.V.B.* p. 493.
2. *W.M.H.S.* Vol. L. p. 309.
3. *O.R.H.S.* Vol. I. p. 504.
4. Conversation with Tom Holland, August 1999.
5. *D.V.B.* pp. 514 & 524.
6. Conversation with Basil Buchanan, June 1999.
7. *D.V.B.* p. 529.
8. A.C.O.T. *Report.* 1982.
9. *D.V.B.* Vol. II, pp. 110 & 113.
10. *Palmerston Estate Papers.* S.C.L L.H.C. Ms. No. F.C./D2/112.
11. *The Sligo Champion.* 27th. August 1979.
12. *D.V.B.* Vol. II, p.41.
13. Joyce Enright: *Introductory Report on the Archaeological Excavation at Drumcliffe Co. Sligo.* 1985. p.7.
14. Report of Archaeologist Valerie J. Keely on the 1999 excavations.

BIBLIOGRAPHY

A) PRIMARY SOURCES
(i) MANUSCRIPT

A List of Persons to whom Premiums for sowing Flax-seed have been adjudged by the Trustees of the Linen Manufacture. S.C.L.L.H.C. Booklet No. 35.

Account Books of the firm of P. Cunningham, Drumcliffe, 1886-1893. S.C.L.L.H.C. Ms. No. 356.

An Chomairle Oiliuna Talmhaiochta: *Agriculture in Co. Sligo.* Sligo 1982. T/S.

Architect's drawing of the new church. Representative Church Boby Library, Dublin.

Books of Survey and Distribution, County Sligo. Details of Forfeited lands under the Act of Settlement, with Explanation. c. 1670. S.C.L.L.H.C. Ms. No. 1214.

Carter, Estella: *The Famine of Co. Sligo, 1845-1847, from Local Newspaper Reports.* S.C.L.L.H.C. No. 72. T/S.

Church of Ireland Parish Registers for Drumcliffe, 1805-1889. S.C.L.L.H.C. Ms. No. 1167.

Cooley, Thomas: *Collection of Drawings.* 1773. Armagh Public Library Ms. No. Z.xxi.33.

Cotton, Don C.F.: *The Heritage of Inishmurray.* T/S. S.C.L.L.H.C. Ms. No.T3.

Curtis,T., Goodwillie, R.& Young R.: *Areas of Scientific Interest in Co. Sligo.* Dublin 1977. T/S. S.C.L.L.H.C. Ms. No. 399.

Diary of Josslyn Gore-Booth. 1894. Private Ms., quoted with permission.

Diary of Thomas Soden, Provost of Sligo, 1787-1818. SC.L.L.H.C. Ms. No. B273.

Elphin Diocesan Census 1749. S.C.L.L.H.C. Ms. No. 331.

Enright, Joyce: *Introductory Report on the Archaeological Excavation at Drumcliffe Co. Sligo,* 1985. T/S. S.C.L.L.H.C. Ms. No. 83.

Griffith Valuation, 1857-58. Vol. xii, Union of Sligo.

Gore-Booth Papers. P.R.O.N.I.

Gray, Edward S.: *Pedigrees of 25 Co. Sligo Families.* 1987. T/S. S.C.L.L.H.C. Ms. No. 284.

Henry, Revd W.: *Hints towards a Natural Topographical History of Sligo.* 1739. P.R.O.I. Ms. No.2533.

Johnston, D.H.G.: *W.B.Yeats and the Gore-Booths at Lissadell.* Unoublished T/S.

King, Bishop Edward: *Visitation of the Diocese of Elphin.* Marsh's Library, Ms. No. 23-1-3.

Leslie, The Revd Chancellor J.B. compiler: *Unpublished Elphin Biographical Succession List.* R.C.B. Library, MS No. 61/2/5.

Leslie, The Revd Chancellor J.B., compiler: *Unpublished Kilmore Biographical Succession List,* R.C.B. Library MS No. 61/2/5.

Letters containing Information relative to the Antiquities of the County of Sligo collected during the progress of the Ordnance Survey in 1836. Reproduced under the direction of Revd M.O'Flanagan. Bray 1928.

Local History Scrapbooks Nos. 1 & 2. S.C.L.L.H.C. Ms. No. 1164.

MacDonagh, J.C.: *Manuscript Collection relating to Antiquities and History of County Sligo and the North-West together with Notes and Pedigrees of Leading Families.* 27 Vols.Vols ii, vi, vii, ix, xiv, xxii & xxiii. S.C.L.L.H.C. Ms. No. 692.

MacManus, Mary G.: *Avowed Happiness of Established Residents In North Sligo, Ireland, with certain changes in Community Life.* University of Manchester M.A. Thesis, 1981. Private T/S.

Minute-Books of Lissadell Select Vestry, 1930 -1996 & 1996-1999. Courtesy of The Select Vestry.

DRUMCLIFFE - The Church of Ireland Parish in its North Sligo Setting.

———— 135 ————

Miscellaneous papers relating to the Parke Family of Dunally 1666-1914.
 S.C.L.L.H.C. Ms. No. 267.
Nimmo, Alexander: *Further Report on the Fishing Station of Mullaghmore in the County of Sligo.* 29 April 1822. S.C.L.L.H.C. Ms. No. 601.
*O'Conor's correspondence with O'Donovan during the 1836 Ordnance Survey.*1836.MS
Palmerston Estate Papers. S.C.L.L.H.C. Ms. No. 555-559.
Pearsall, A.W.H., National Maritime Museum Historian,
 Letter to John McTernan concerning *The Pomona.*
Petrie, George: Journal of a Tour in Co. Sligo. 1837. S.C.L.L.H.C. Ms. No.1281.
Raftery, Joyce: *Preliminary Report on Sites of Archaeological Interest in Co. Sligo.*
 Dublin 1974. T/S. S.C.L.L.H.C. Booklet No.121.
Register of Motor-Cars, December 1903-January 1921. S.C.L.L.H.C. Ms. L.706.
Religious Census of the Diocese of Elphin. 1766. National Archive, Ms No. MFS6.
Report of Crash of Flying Fortress, Military Archives, Cathal Brugha Barracks. T/S. Ms.
 No. G2-X-125.
Report of Sligo Field Club to National Monuments Advisory Council Dublin. T/S. 1904.
 S.C.L.L.H.C. Ms. No. 50.
Ryan, Deirdre: *Sir Robert Gore-Booth - Famine and Emigration, 1845-1847.*
 U.C.D. M.A. Thesis 1996.
Seventeenth Century Hearth Money Rolls with Full Transcript Relating to County Sligo, ed.
 Edward Mac Lysaght. S.C.L.L.H.C. Ms. No. 1219.
Survey and Rentals of Lands in County Sligo in the 17th and 18th Centuries.
 MacDonagh Ms. xiii.
Townlands of County Sligo by Civil Parish (with accompanying maps.) Sligo 1987.
 AnCo Project. S.C.L.L.H.C. Ms. No. T1.
Traynor, Revd Owen Francis: *'Calendar of MacDonagh Mss.'* In Local History Handbook,
 available at counter, Sligo County Library.
Vestry Book of Drumcliffe Parish 1756-1970. Courtesy of the Rector.
Vestry Book of Drumcliffe,1970 to the Present Day. Courtesy of the Rector.
Wagner, W.E.(compiler): *History and Succession-list of the Clergy of Elphin.*
 Armagh Public Library Ms. No. K.H.i.15.
Walker of Rathcarrick, Roger Chambers: *Account Book.* S.C.L.L.H.C. Ms. No. 575.
Wynne Papers. Private collection, also at P.R.O.N.I.

(ii) PRINTED

Alemande, L.A.: *Monasticon Hibernicum or the Monastical History of Ireland* London 1722.
Annals of Boyle, The. Ed. John D'Alton. Vols I & II. Dublin 1845.
Annals of Clonmacnoise, The: tr. Conall McGeoghagan. Dublin 1896.
Annals of Connaught, The, A.D. 1224-1544. ed. A. Martin Freeman. Dublin 1970.
Annals of the Four Masters, The: Ed. John O'Donovan. Dublin 1851.
Annals of Inisfallen, The. Ed, & tr. Sean MacAirt. Dublin 1977.
Annals of Lough Ce, The: ed. William M. Hennessy, in 2 Vols. London 1871.
Annals of Tigernach, The: ed. Dennis Murphy. Llanerch 1993.
Annals of Ulster, The: ed, & tr. William M. Hennessy & B. MacCarthy. Dublin 1887.
Archdall, Mervyn: *Monasticon Hibernicum.* Dublin 1786.
Binns, Jonathan: *The Miseries and Beauties of Ireland.* London 1837.
Bowe, Nicola Gordon, Caron, David & Wynne, Michael: *Gazetteer of Irish Stained Glass.*

Blackrock 1988.

Crockford's Clerical Directory for 1883. London 1883.

Church Directory for 1865, The: Dublin 1865.

Cumin, Patrick: *Report of the Royal Commission of Enquiry into Primary Education, Ireland.* 1870.

Curwen, J.C.: *Observations on the State of Ireland Principally Directed to its Agriculture and Rural Population in a Series of Letters Written on a Tour Through that Country.* In 2 vols. London 1818.

Drumcliffe G.A.A. 1888-1988. Drumcliffe 1988. S.C.L.L.H.C. Ms. No. S506.

List of Transatlantic Sailings 1803-1855 as per Local Newspapers. T/S. S.C.L.L.H.C. Ms. No. E 506.

Foley, Gerry: *A Historical Report on the Gleniff (Barytes) Steam Mill.* Ballintrillick 1998.

Foster, Thomas Campbell: *Letters on the Condition of the People of Ireland.* London 1846.

Fraser, James: *A Handbook for travellers in Ireland.* Dublin 1844.

Griffith, Richard: *General Valuation of Ireland:* County Sligo. 1843.

Inglis, Henry D.: *A Journey throughout Ireland during the Spring, Summer and Autumn of 1834.* London 1836.

Irish Ecclesiastical Gazette, The: 1890 & 1895.

Irwin, Henry, M.D.: *A Record of the Cholera Asiatica as it occurred in Sligo in the months of August and September 1832.* Sligo 1832.

Joyce, P.W.: *The Origin and History of Irish Names of Places,*2nd. Edn.Dublin 1870.

Martyrology of Donegal, the- A Calendar of the Saints of Ireland: ed. & tr. J.H.Todd & William Reeves. Dublin 1864.

Martyrology of Oengus the Culdee, The: ed. & tr. Whitley Stokes. 2nd. Edn. London 1905.

Martyrology of Tallaght, The, from The Book of Leinster: ed. R.H.Best & Hugh Jackson Lawlor. London 1931.

O'Donnell, Manus: *Betha Colum Chille,* ed. A. O'Kelleher & G. Schoepperle. Illinois 1918.

Parliamentary Gazetteer of Ireland, The: Dublin 1846.

Sligo Champion, The. Various years. (1979, 1898, etc.)

Tripartite Life of Patrick, The: ed. Kathleen Mulchrone. Dublin 1939.

Survey and Distribution Books, 1637. Sligo County Library.

Ware, Sir James: *The History of the Bishops.* In: The Whole Works of Sir James Ware concerning Ireland, in 2 Vols. Dublin 1764. With annotations by Walter Harris.

Wynne, Arthur F.G.S. and Bailey W.H. F.G.S.: *Explanatory Memoir to Accompany Sheets 42 & 43 of the maps of the Geological Survey of Ireland comprising the Counties of Sligo and Leitrim.* 1885.

Yeats, W.B.: *Memoirs,* ed. Denis Donoghue. London 1972.

Yeats, W.B.: *Reveries over Childhood and Youth.* Dundrum 1915.

Young Arthur: ed. Arthur Wollaston Hutton: *Arthur Young's Tour of Ireland, 1776-1779.* London 1982.

(B) SECONDARY SOURCES

Acheson, Alan: *A History of the Church of Ireland, 1691-1996.* Dublin 1997.

Anderson, A.O. & M.O.: *Adomnan's Life of Columba.* London 1961.

Ardill, Rev. John Roche: *St. Patrick A.D.180.* London 1931.

Ardill, Rev. John Roche: *Forgotten Facts of Irish History.* Dublin 1905.

Bence-Jones, Mark: *A Guide to Irish Country Houses. Revised Edition.* London 1988.

Binns, Jonathan: *The Miseries and Beauties of Ireland.* London 1837.

Bolger, Patrick: *The Irish Co-operative Movement - its History and Development.* Dublin 1977.

Bradley, Ian: *Columba - Pilgrim and Penitent.* Glasgow 1996.

Burke, Sir Bernard: *A Genealogical and Heraldic Dictionary of the Peerage and Baronetage.* London 1901.

Burke, Sir Bernard: *A Genaeological and Heraldic History of the Landed Gentry of Great Britain and Ireland.* London 1894.

Byrne, Francis J.: *Irish Kings and High Kings.* London 1973.

Coote, Stephen: *W.B. Yeats - A Life.* London 1997.

Cowell, John: *Land of Yeats' Desire.* Revised Edition. Dublin 1997.

Cusack, Mary Frances: *An Illustrated History of Ireland from A.D. 400-1800.* New Edition. London 1995.

De Paor, Maire & Liam: *Early Christian Ireland.* London 1958.

Dickson, David: *Arctic Ireland.* Belfast 1997.

Dingfelder, Dorothy Rines, arr.: *Schoolmasters and Schoolmistresses in Co. Sligo Ireland, 826-1827, Extracted from Parochial Returns.* Report to the Commission for Education, 1981.

Eccles, Jan: *A Twentieth Century Life in Ireland.* Coleraine. 1996.

Finnegan, T.A.: *Rosses Point and Coney Island.* Sligo 1977.

Flanagan, Laurence: *Irish Wrecks of the Spanish Armada.* Dublin 1995.

Fuller, J.F.: *Pedigree of the Family of Ormsby formerly of Lincolnshire, now of Ireland.* London 1886.

Gallagher, D., et al: *Seventeenth Century Sligo.* F.A.S./S.F.H.R.S. project. S.C.L.L.H.C. Booklet No. 49. T/S.

Gallagher, Dara: *The Pursuit of Diarmaid and Grainne.* T/S. S.C.L.L.H.C. Ms. H.62.

Gore-Booth, Eva: *Poems of Eva Gore-Booth with a Biographical Introduction by Esther Roper.* London 1929.

Gore-Booth, Paul: *With Great Truth and Respect.* London 1974.

Guthrie-Jones, Winston: *The Wynnes of Sligo and Leitrim.* Manorhamilton 1994.

Gwynne, Aubrey & Hadcock, R. Neville: *Mediaeval Religious Houses - Ireland.* London 1970.

Haran, Majella: *The Gore Family in Seventeenth Century Ireland.* Ms. S.C.L.L.H.C. Ms. No. 287.

Harbison, Peter: *High Crosses of Ireland.* 2 Vols. Bonn 1992.

Haverty, Anne: *Constance Markievicz - An Independent Life.* London 1988.

Hayes, R.J.: *Manuscript Sources for the History of Irish Civilization.* Boston 1965.

Helferty, Seamus & Refaussee, Raymond, ed.: *Directory of Irish Archives.* Second Edition. Dublin 1993.

Heraughty, Patrick: *Inishmurray - Ancient Monastic Island.* Revised Edn. Dublin 1982.

Hough, Richard: *Mountbatten - Hero of our Time.* London 1980.

Hyde, Douglas: *A Literary History of Ireland.* London 1910.

Jope, E.M.: *Studies in Building History.* London 1961.

Joyce, P.W.: *A Short History of Ireland from the Earliest Times to 1608.* London 1904.

Kenny, Colum: *Molaise - Abbot of Leighlin and Hermit of Holy Island.* Killala 1998.

Kilgannon, Tadhg: *Sligo and its Surroundings.* Sligo 1926.

Killanin, Lord & Duignan, Michael V.: *Shell Guide to Ireland.* London 1962.

Kirby, Sheelah (Compiler) & Gallagher, Patrick (ed.). *The Yeats Country.* Dublin 1962.

Kirby, Sheelah: *A Guide to Drumcliffe.*(undated).

Lane-Poole, Stanley: *North-West and By North.* Dublin 1903.

Legg, Marie-Louise, ed.: *The Synge Letters - Bishop Edward Synge to his Daughter Alicia, Roscommon to Dublin 1746-1752.* Dublin 1996.

Lewis, Samuel: *A Topographical Dictionary of Ireland.* London 1837.

Loane, Erica: *Architectural Drawings by Thomas Cooley in the Public Library Armagh.* 1983. Undergraduate Thesis, History of Art Dept. T.C.D. Armagh Public Library Ms. No. L.B.I:15.

Logan, Patrick: *The Holy Wells of Ireland.* Gerrards Cross 1980.

McElhone, Patricia: *Lift the Latch - Memories of Old Rosses Point.* Tralee, c.1994.

McGowan, Joe: *Inishmurray - Gale, Stone and Fire.* Mullaghmore 1998.

McGowan, Joe: *In the Shadow of Benbulben.* Mullaghmore 1993.

MacGregor, Duncan: *Saint Columba - a Record and a Tribute.* Aberdeen 1898.

McHale, J, et al: *Eighteenth Century Sligo.* F.A.S./S.F.H.R.S. project. S.C.L.L.H.C. Booklet No. 49. T/S.

MacManus, Seamus: *The Story of the Irish Race.* Revised Edition, New York 1966.

McTernan, John C.: *Historic Sligo.* Sligo 1965.

McTernan, John C.: *In Sligo Long Ago - Aspects of Town and County over Two Centuries.* Sligo 1998.

McTernan, John C.: *Notes on Bartholomew Teeling.* TS. S.C.L.L.H.C. Ms.No. 190.

McTernan, John C.: *Olde Sligoe - aspects of Town and County over 750 Years.* Sligo 1997.

McTernan, John C.,ed.: *Sligo Sources of Local History.* Sligo 1994.

Manning, Robert: *Report to the Commissioners appointed under the above acts, on the Drainage and Improvement of the lands in the above district* (Drumcliffe). Dublin 1847.

Markus, Gilbert, O.P.: *Adomnan's Law of the Innocents.* Glasgow 1997.

Marreco, Anne: *The Rebel Countess - The Life and Times of Constance Markievicz.* London 1967.

Marsden, John: *The Illustrated Life of Columba.* Revised Edition. Edinburgh 1995.

Mason, Thomas H.: *The Islands of Ireland.* Cork, 1919.

Montalembert, Count de: *Saint Columba - Apostle of Caledonia.* Edinburgh 1868.

Moody, T.W. & Martin, F.X.: *The Course of Irish History.* Revised Edition, Cork 1994.

Mountbatten, Earl: *A Short History of Classiebawn Castle.* (Private photocopy, used with permission).

Murphy, William M.: *The Yeats Family and the Pollexfens of Sligo.* Dublin 1971.

Nicholls, Kenneth: *Gaelic and Gaelicised Ireland in the Middle Ages.* Dublin 1972.

O'Croinin, Daibhi: *Early Mediaeval Ireland 400-1200.* Harlow 1995.

O'Hart, John: *Irish Pedigrees - or The Origin and Stem of the Irish Nation.* New York 1923.

O'Rorke, T.: *The History of Sligo Town and County.* Vols. I & II. Dublin 1890.

Perceval-Maxwell, M.: *The Outbreak of the Irish Rebellion of 1641.* Dublin 1994.

Phillips, Walter Alison: *History of the Church of Ireland.* Vol. III. Oxford 1933.

Praeger, Robert Lloyd: *The Way that I Went.* Dublin 1969.

Pyle, Hilary: *Red-Headed Rebel.* Susan L. Mitchell, Poet amd Mystic of the Irish Cultural Renaissance. Dublin 1998.

Quinn, Bob: *Atlantean - Ireland's North African and Maritime Heritage.* London 1986.

Quinn, Rev. M.: *St. Molaise's Park Grange.* Sligo 1985.

Reeves, W.: *The Life of St. Columba* (Adomnan). Edinburgh 1874.

Richardson, Hilary R. & Scarry, John: *An Introduction to Irish High Crosses.* Cork 1990.

Roper, Esther: *Prison Letters of Countess Markievicz*. London 1987.
Rosenthal, T.G.: *Yeats*. In 'The Masters' series. No. 40. Bristol 1963.
Ryan, John S.J.: *Irish Monasticism - Origins and Early Development*.
    Second Edition, Dublin 1972.
Salter, M.: *Castles and Stronghouses of Ireland*. Malvern 1993.
Simms, George Otto: *The Psalms in the time of St. Columba*. Dublin 1963.
Simpson, W. Douglas: *The Historical St. Columba*. Aberdeen 1927.
Stalley. Roger: *Irish High Crosses*. Dublin 1996.
Toher, Tony: *Exploring Sligo and North Leitrim*. Sligo 1994.
Tunney, John: *Saint Colmcille and the Columban Heritage*. Donegal 1987.
Waddell, John: *The Prehistoric Archaeology of Ireland*. Galway 1998.
Wanchope, Piers A.C.: *Patrick Sarsfield and the Williamite War*. Blackrock 1992.
Wood-Martin, W.G.: *History of Sligo, County and Town*. Vols. I, II & III. Dublin 1892.
Wood-Martin, W.G.: *Sligo and the Enniskilleners from 1688-1691*. Dublin 1880.
Wood-Martin, W.G.: *The Lake Dwellings of Ireland - or Ancient Lacustrine Habitations of Erin -*
    commonly called Crannogs. Dublin 1886.
Yeats, W.B.: *Autobiographies*. London 1955.
Yeats, W.B.: *Letters*. In Collected Letters of W.B.Yeats ed. John Kelly & Guy Domville.
    London 1986.

ARTICLES

Anon. 'Notes of Home Rambles'. *The Irish Monthly*, 1883.
Bourke, Cormac: 'A Crozier and Bell from Inishmurray and their Place in Ninth Century
Irish Archaeology'. *P.R.I.A.*, Vol. 85, C, No. 5, 1985.
Burchell, J.T.: 'The Sligo Archaeological Discovery'. *The Catholic Bulletin,*Vol 18. 1928.
Burns, Ann: 'Rural Life Seventy Years Ago'. Undated. S.C.L.L.H.C. Ms No.H39.
Connellan, M.: 'St. Muadhnat of Kill Muadhnat'. *G.A.S.J.* Vol. XXI. 1944-5, pp.56-62.
Cotton, Don: 'Sligo's Undiscovered Wild Places'. *L.H.* Vol. 9, No. 1, Spring/Summer 1992.
French, J. Allen: 'Notes and Queries on a Souterraine at Drumcliff Co, Sligo'.
    J.R.S.A.I., 1885.
De Valera, R.: 'The Court Cairns of Ireland'. *P.R.I.A.* 1960.
Hencken, H. O'Neill: 'A Long Cairn at Creevykeel Co. Sligo'.
    J.R.S.A.I., Vol. LXIX, pt.II, 1939.
Irish Homestead, The. May 1895. Report on the inauguration of Drumcliffe Co-operative
    Dairy Society.
Jennings, A.G.: 'Barytes Development in Sligo'. *Bulletin of the Institute of Civil Engineers of*
    Ireland, Vol. 73. 1946-1947. Dublin
Kelly, Rev. J.J.: 'Saint Assicus and Patron Saints of the Diocese of Elphin'.
    *I.E.R.,*Vol. 14, 1893.
MacConnell, Cormac: 'Surf and Turf - Where and How to cut Turf at Sea!'.
    Ireland of the Welcomes, Vol.42 No. 5. Sept.-Oct. 1993.
McGrath, Walter: 'Some Industrial Railways of Ireland'. *The Irish Railway Record Society*,
    1958.
Mentbert, Coquebert de: 'A Frenchman's Tour in Connaught 1791'.
    G.A.S.J. tr. Sile Ni Chinneide.
Milligan, Seaton F.: 'Ancient Forts in Co. Sligo'. *J.R.S.A.I.* Vol. 21, 1890/1891, pp. 574-582.

Morris, Henry: 'Benbulbin in History and Literature'. Undated pamphlet printed by
    The Sligo Champion, c. 193-. S.C.L.L.H.C. Ms. 700.

Morris, Henry: 'Dun na mBarc and the Lady Ceasair'. *J.R.S.A.I.*, 1933, pp. 69-87.

Morris, Henry: 'Researches in Local History'. Selection of articles in Local Newpapers.
    S.C.L.L.H.C. Booklet No. 27.

O'Driscoll, Denis: 'Salmon of the Ballisodare and Drumcliffe Rivers'.
    Scientific Proceedings of the Royal Irish Academy, 1950.

O'Reilly, J.P.: 'Remarks on Certain Passages in Capt. Cuellar's Narrative of his
    Adventures in Ireland after the Wreck of the Spanish Armada in 1588-89,
    followed by a Literal Translation of that Narrative'. *P.R.I.A.* Dec. 1893.

Stokes, Margaret: 'Notes on the High Cross of Drumcliffe'. Transactions of the Royal Irish
    Academy. Dublin 1901.

Timoney, Martin A.: 'Recently Discovered High Cross at Drumcliff, Co. Sligo'.
    The Corran Herald. Issue No. 32, 1999/2000.

Wakeman, W.F.: 'Notice of the Architectural Peculiarities of some Ancient Churches in
    County Sligo'. *P.R.H.A.A.I.* 1886.

Wakeman, W.F.:'On Certain Wells Situate in the North-West of Ireland, with Remarks on
    the Occurrence of the croix gammee or swastica, as found at St. Brigid's Well
    near Cliffoney Co. Sligo'. *J.R.S.A.I.* 1880, pp. 18ff.

Wakeman, W.F.: 'The Oaken Statue of St. Molaise on Inishmurray'.In "Graves of
    Illustrious Irishmen". *Joly Pamphlet* No. 1829.

Willis, David: 'New Roles for Old Houses - Country Houses of Sligo'. *L.H.* Vol IX. 1992.

Wood, Cornet Richard: 'Account of the Protestant Association Meeting at Sligo,1688'.
    G.A.S.J. 1944/5.

INDEX